Making Chaplaincy Work: Practical Approaches

Making Chaplaincy Work: Practical Approaches

Laurel Arthur Burton
Editor

The Haworth Press
New York • London

Making Chaplaincy Work: Practical Approaches has also been published as *Journal of Health Care Chaplaincy*, Volume 1, Number 2, Spring/Summer 1988

The Haworth Press, Inc. 10 Alice Street, Binghamton, NY 13904-1580
EUROSPAN/Haworth, 3 Henrietta Street, London WC2E 8LU England

LIBRARY OF CONGRESS
Library of Congress Cataloging-in-Publication Data

Making chaplaincy work : practical approaches / Laurel Arthur Burton, editor.
    p.   cm.
    "Has also been published as Journal of health care chaplaincy, volume 1, number 2, spring/
summer 1988" — T.p. verso
    Includes bibliographies.
    ISBN 0-86656-743-7
    1. Chaplains, Hospital. I. Burton, Laurel Arthur. BV4335.M34 1988
259'.4 — dc19   88-541
                                                                      CIP

Making Chaplaincy Work: Practical Approaches

CONTENTS

**The Use of Volunteer Community Clergy as Hospital
Pastoral Care Staff**   **91**
Dale E. Guckenberger, MDiv

ABOUT THE EDITOR

Laurel Arthur Burton, ThD, is Head of the Department of Pastoral Care, Counseling, and Education at Boston University Medical Center. He is a supervisor with the Association for Clinical Pastoral Education, a member of the American Association of Pastoral Counselors, a clinical member of the American Association for Marriage and Family Therapy, and a Fellow in the College of Chaplains. He has published articles on bioethics, popular culture, pastoral care and counseling, as well as short stories and numerous book reviews. Dr. Burton earned his Doctor of Theology degree at Boston University School of Theology and is ordained in the United Methodist Church. He is the editor of the *Journal of Health Care Chaplaincy*.

Introduction

Chaplaincy was, in many ways, born of need and nurtured by practice. Since the earliest days of professional health care chaplaincy in America, members of our profession have drawn the theory of our work from experiences of daily praxis. Chaplaincy has always been, then, intensely practical.

This volume of articles, contributed by practicing chaplains, draws on a wide range of experience and seeks to point to principles, themes, or guidelines others of us can use to enhance our own ministries. The first two contributors are members of the Editorial Committee of the *Journal of Health Care Chaplaincy*. Larry VandeCreek, active in research in the ACPE as well as AAPC, is a member of the faculty at the Medical School at Ohio State. He illustrates some basic principles for the chaplain as ethicist in the midst of institutional cost cutting/containment. Daniel G. Kratz is a busy chaplaincy executive and practitioner, working with a large corporation specializing in long term care. He lifts up some simple, but important, guidelines for work with people in institutions such as his.

Robert D. Craig, a staff chaplain at Methodist Medical Center in Peoria, and a Fellow in the College of Chaplains, has presented workshops about the integrated way chaplains work with a surgical team, and here illustrates their method and offers his own version of "10 Commandments." Richard J. Gerber, a CPE Supervisor in Minnesota, illustrates his conception of the tensions in decision-making by/with terminally ill people, with material from his work at Mercy Medical Center.

In 1986 the first World Council of Churches Consultation on AIDS was held in Geneva. Charles W. Kessler, whose major work is now with AIDS patients, was invited to present one of the papers, which is included here with stories of some of the people with whom he has worked. While doing a CPE residency, Sr. Cecilia Baranowski began her study of patients who had suffered strokes. Her experience began as these patients were hospitalized and continued into rehabilitation and nursing home settings. She is presently at St. Anne's Hospital in Fall River, MA. Finally, a colleague from the College of Chaplains, Dale Guckenberger, convened a session at the 1987 convention about the use of volunteers. Out of that meeting he made a further survey of how volunteer chaplains are used in a variety of institutions.

All of us in health care chaplaincy face professional challenges every day. Gathered here are some of the practical approaches that make chaplaincy work for some of our colleagues. I hope these work for you, too.

Laurel Arthur Burton, ThD
Editor

The Chaplain as Hospital Ethicist in the Cost Containment Struggle

Larry VandeCreek, DMin

SUMMARY. How can quality health care be maintained in the era of cost containment? This article argues that allegiance to relevant ethical principles at the root of the health care process is necessary and that the chaplain can make an important contribution by discussing them within the institution. This article seeks to be a resource to such discussions and presents three fundamental ethical assumptions and three specific principles which can aid in shaping the health care cost containment struggle. Case studies are provided as a context for the ethical principles.

INTRODUCTION

Money drives the health care system. Physicians and hospitals, indeed the entire industry, can create radically new practices when these increase their fiscal standing. Not many years ago patients remained in the hospital for days and weeks because their physicians judged it too dangerous for them to return home. Today it is different. Patients experience "same day surgery" and mothers return home with their newborns 48 hours after delivery.

These and other changes are, at least in part, due to health care cost containment efforts by Medicare and other private insurance carriers. Hospitals are now paid a predetermined amount for specific patient diagnoses without regard to the length of stay and,

Larry VandeCreek, Assistant Professor, Department of Family Medicine, Ohio State University Columbus, OH 43210.

The original research for this article was conducted for the Health Care Cost Containment Public Policy Panel and the Commission on Interprofessional Education and Practice at the Ohio State University. Results of this research are also found in Chapter 5 of the Panel's report.

3

consequently, rapid hospital discharge lessens expenditures, increasing profits. In this instance as well as others, money determines medical practices.

These cost containment efforts and their consequent changes in medical practices raise important ethical problems. A forthcoming Report will diagnose these problems as centering on issues of health care quality, noting that a decrease in quality is always a tempting way to cut costs. The Report will go on to say that quality is concrete and measurable, composed of 5 "A"'s: availability, accountability, accessibility, affordability, and affability (Health Care Cost Containment Public Policy Panel, 1987).

How can the system maintain quality health care in the face of cost cutting measures? It can be maintained by allegiance to relevant ethical principles buried beneath the surface of the health care process. The moral quality of changes in medical practice can be discerned only when these basic ethical principles are uncovered and valued. Without such rootage, the health care process in the United States will become totally entrepreneurial with an ethical system like that of the marketplace. Hospital chaplains can make an important contribution within their institutions by dissecting emerging patterns of practice and pointing to fundamental ethical principles.

This article is intended as a resource to hospital chaplains who wish to make such a contribution. I will comment first on the existing literature. Second, I will discuss the contribution and limits of ethics in this area of health care. Third, I will describe three fundamental ethical assumptions which form the underpinnings of health care. Finally, I will elaborate, within the context of brief case studies, three specific ethical principles which can aid us in the cost containment effort.

LITERATURE

The background to our current health care cost dilemmas lies deep in Western culture's determination to become scientific. Until the opening of the 20th century, physicians possessed few curative measures and scientific interventions were limited. Ethical dilemmas existed but religious and cultural solutions had been developed over the centuries. The ethical literature of this period usually sought to justify the status quo.

Scientific medicine as it grew after the Flexner Report created many new curative measures, including the discovery and clinical use of x-rays, antibiotics, and advanced surgical techniques (Flexner, 1910). These as well as other advances occasioned unique ethical problems or sharpened existing ones. These advances brought with them not only power and expenditure of money but also expectations from the public. These expectations gradually crystallized into an implicit sense that individuals possessed an ethical right to health care. These developments, in part, led the President's Commission on Health Needs of the Nation to state in 1953, "access to the means for the attainment and preservation of health is a basic human right" (President's Commission, 1953).

Three decades later another presidential commission exhaustively examined ethical issues in health care and spoke in terms of "ethical obligations" (of society) rather than "rights" (of individuals). Their multi-volume report contains the largest single current bank of material concerning ethical issues in health care and is a valuable resource. Reference to ethical issues abound in these volumes. Persons further interested in these issues will find three chapters of particular interest (President's Commission, 1983). Some of that material is reflected below.

Another major resource consists of the National Heart Transplantation Study. Three chapters are devoted to ethical issues but no reference is made to constraining costs although the kindred issue of scarce resources allocation is discussed in detail (Evans, 1984).

Authors have addressed cost containment problems in individual articles and a computerized literature search on the Health Planning and Administration data base of MEDLARS revealed some of these (Abram and Wolf, 1984; Bayer et al., 1983; Wanzer et al., 1984; Culliton, 1986; Kapp, 1984; Kapp, 1985; Blendon and Altman, 1984).

THE CONTRIBUTION
AND LIMITATIONS OF ETHICS

Ethics studies morals, that is, the actual beliefs and practices concerning right and wrong. Morals have, of course, been with us since the human race began. The content of ethics, as begun in ancient philosophy, is the formal discipline of thinking systematically about what is right and wrong, good and bad.

Many of the basic ethical issues and dilemmas remain the same from the beginning. Martin Marty reports an anecdote concerning theology and philosophy which, when applied to ethics, illustrates the point. An American visitor toured the University of Gottingen after World War II. A German physicist acting as tour guide boasted about the past scientific glories of the University and the bright future. The visitor asked why the University's past glories in religious and philosophical thought went unmentioned. The physicist dismissed their inquiry. "Oh theology and philosophy," he said, "They'll never discover anything new over there" (Marty, 1986).

What then is the contribution of ethics if they "never discover anything new over there"? The contribution is that of providing a framework within which to discuss the "good" and "right" use of human advancements and technology. As many have discovered in this nuclear age, innocent discoveries envisioned for the betterment of the human condition can be turned to evil ends. Technology in itself does not contain values; values are attributed by society and individual users. Ethics speaks to the "goodness" or the "badness" to which we put our advancements. And such advancements always challenge ethics to refine the meaning of its principles in ways which are applicable to the advancements. Ethics therefore will not make discoveries but will guide the use of these advancements through its principles and their application. Both ancient and modern humans are concerned to maintain many of the same moral rules, i.e., you must tell the truth; you must not kill another human being. And yet, "You must not kill" has become more complicated since technology created unique opportunities to keep bodies breathing indefinitely. The contribution of ethics, therefore, is not that of new discovery but of redefining and shaping old principles.

The ethics perspective can make one additional contribution. Given its focus on what is "right" and "good," ethics can ask penetrating questions of and make incisive observations about society and its sense of what is "good" and "right." Such *post hoc* analyses serve to critique society as well as its professions and call them to account for consequences of their assumptions. This may be the role of ethics in cost containment efforts.

While this contribution is critically important, some may not regard it as substantial because it does not recommend specific actions. Ethics, at least in the context of this study, cannot become concretely prescriptive. In the remainder of this article, I will discuss societal and individual danger points and describe responses which can guide the health care cost containment effort. This leaves specific details to program planners, politicians, and the various health care system constituents.

This approach uncovers fundamental assumptions and produces useful principles, principles which some will find so elementary as to need no discussion. They will be tempted to lose interest. And yet, these basic assumptions and principles are constantly in danger of being overlooked and neglected in favor of specific pragmatic and self-serving solutions.

CONTRIBUTIONS

Fundamental Ethical Assumptions

In this section I will discuss three selected ethical assumptions which lie at the foundation of health care.

The first assumption is: the well-being of individuals and society must be promoted by health care. This is a traditional assumption in health care and three observations are necessary. First, the emphasis is on well-being, healthfulness. Society is struggling to acknowledge that helping people keep well is highly valuable, believing that "an ounce of prevention is worth a pound of cure." Solid progress is being made in some circles, but much more is needed. Society still believes in the "illness model." This model is found in the general public's fantasy that persons can live as they please without consequences and, when illness strikes, no precursors are involved. The medical profession has extended this public assumption into its own allocation of time and energy in which sick persons receive more interest and attention than preventive measures. Dramatic diagnostic and treatment intervention into the maladies of the sick are certainly exciting but they are always "after the fact," after disease has struck. The fundamental mission of health care is a broad-based well-being in which disease is prevented as well as cured.

Second, this first concept emphasizes well-being rather than economic pragmatism. Health care must promote the well-being of individuals and society rather than the self-interests of providers and payers. Health care is composed of service professions. The purpose here is not to determine if providers and payers serve their self-interest too frequently; it is necessary, however, to point out that the pressure to practice money-making-medicine is ever present and sometimes subtle. Sometimes it is blatant. In either instance it flies in the face of this assumption and is unethical. This natural temptation toward human greed justifies review mechanisms such as audit and quality assurance measures. The current need for cost containment is doubtlessly due to many factors but one important reason is inadequate attention to this ethical principle which emphasizes the service aspects of the health care professions rather than income for providers and payers.

A final observation is necessary concerning this first assumption. The health care rights, privileges, and benefits of patients and the total society are often similar and without conflict. For example, both individuals and society benefited from discovery and use of vaccines. Ethical issues arise however, when the well-being of individuals and society conflict. For example, must public monies supply the most expensive specialized hospital intensive care facilities for every patient with coronary disease? When shortage of this resource occurs, how is rationing of the usage determined? Some balance must be found between the interests of society and the individual patient. Financial concerns legitimately make their way into these decisions, but from an ethics point of view, they cannot become the dominant element in decision making. The dominant theme in the containment of health care cost must continue to be the well-being of individuals and society, discovering an acceptable balance when these latter two conflict.

The second assumption is: doctors and patients alike must show respect for and build upon the relational nature of health care delivery. This has far reaching implications.

Providing and receiving health care is done through human relationships. The doctor-patient relationship is at the core of health care and the expectations of that relationship are central. Health care happens when the relationship fosters the patient's openness and trust as well as the physician's confidence and beneficence. The more chronic the illness, the more important the doctor-patient relationship becomes. The more emphasis placed on prevention, the more the doctor-patient relationship is central. Human nature being as it is, however, the patient who does not like the doctor is tempted to ignore the advice. Equally so, the doctor who does not like the patient can soon slip into performing less than quality care. The containment of health care cost, therefore, cannot ignore the doctor-patient relationship because a problematic relationship always seems to lead to higher costs. From an ethics point of view, therefore, it is wrong to curtail cost by compromising the relationship between doctor and patient.

Unfortunately this central relationship feature is already compromised in our current system. Financial rewards in the medical profession go to those who can do a procedure, a technical process, rather than to those who carefully build a relationship by talking with the patient. In fact, such relational activities are penalized because as physicians talk with patients, they lose income available from another patient on whom he could have performed a procedure.

In this way, the increasing health care technology is often an enemy of the doctor-patient relationship. This technology has grown in geometric proportions and has almost completely taken over in some medical specialties. Specialists in these areas are tempted to neglect the relationship to the patient and to accent the procurement of subjects on whom the procedures can be performed and the fees collected, sometimes announcing the results to the patient but more often to other specialists. In some of these instances, society must ask the specialists whether any health care was delivered, whether any good occurred to the patient, whether any benefit resulted besides paying for the technology and those involved with it. From a health care ethics point of view, such activity is good only after clear demonstration that the patient benefits.

Many examples of technology's increasing dominance exists, including the resultant problems in the doctor-patient relationship. An example is the repeated cardiac resuscitation of terminally ill patients. This issue is receiving wide public and professional discussion because the use of technology became so absurd in some quarters that review was inevitable (Huttman, 1983). The doctor-patient relationship (or relationship to the family if the patient is comatose) must be the vehicle for the necessary decision making. No doubt the doctor must frequently lead the way in constructing the relationship, and often suggest treatment interventions. Physicians must not confuse this initiative, however, with the patient's (or family's) need to be involved in the decision making. The physician's initiative must not be understood as the right to autocratic decisions. Such an autocratic style will inevitably lead to excessive self-interest and increased cost. In this example as in any other, the premier issue is the delivery of health care through the doctor-patient relationship, a relationship which uses technology when appropriate.

The largest ethical concern here, therefore, moves to the very identity of the medical profession. Is medicine a profession based on moral qualities of trust, altruism, scholarship and respect worked out in a relationship between doctor and patient, or is it a trade in the marketplace which applies technologies and procedures whenever possible? The struggle is insidious and the balance has tilted toward the latter in the last 25 years. Deep foundations of medicine as a classical profession remain but these will continue to erode unless future generations of physicians can counteract the pressure to practice money-making medicine by simply performing technological procedures.

One final aspect of this key concept with its ethical implications remains to be discussed. We have discussed up to this point the pressures on and the ethical dilemmas of the physician. Relationships, however, are always reciprocal and health care delivery is no exception. The patient, as individual, family, or society, also has ethical obligations and they must shoulder some responsibilities for the current cost containment problems.

Relationships always carry expectations and the patient who seeks health care is filled with them. Naming and numbering these patient expectations are endless but it is clear that some (perhaps many) expectations are unreasonable. Many patients, according to compliance studies, come to the physician but do not invest in the relationship or follow the advice. Some never intend to follow a physician's advice, seeking physician contact for a multitude of covert reasons. Such covert reasons are not unethical (i.e., bad/wrong) until they impinge on the well-being of the patient, the family, the physician, or society. This appears to happen with increasing frequency and intensity. Indeed, one way to manage the current need for health care cost containment is to be more clear about inappropriate use of the health care system by patients and society. If the physician's duty is to build a help-providing relationship with the patient, the patient's duty is to participate appropriately in that relationship and make use of the expert advice.

The most global manifestation of unrealistic expectations is society's temptation to select specific professions for deliverance from all that is wrong. This process is as old as human history itself. Society and its individuals pin hopes for answers to life's puzzles on others, searching for utopia. The church was the recipient of this hope for many centuries. Other institutions or professions chosen by society included education (particularly at the high school and then the college level), government, and the social welfare movement. Society did not ask whether such expectations were appropriate or realistic. Understandably, society eventually turned away in disappointment, frustration, and disillusionment. For many persons in our culture, the health care system epitomized by physicians has been the focus for such exaggerated and unrealistic dreams in this century. As with the church and education, this attention spanned a "golden age" which then passed as society turned away, looking elsewhere for answers. In this way society, in its broadest search for utopia, placed unfair demands and expected unrealistic results from the health care system. The medical literature is already asking whether the golden age of medicine is gone (Burnham, 1982). This is more than a wishing for "the good old days." It is an awareness that medicine as a profession is being watched, scrutinized, criticized and in some cases debunked and ridiculed. Similar processes involving disillusionment have occurred with the church, education, and social welfare. While there are many reasons for the current mounting malpractice crisis, it appears that, at least in part, patients and their families are going after physicians with a vengeance born of dashed utopian expectations and hopes.

The point here is that society and individual patients must increasingly shoulder the responsibility for their unrealistic expectations of their physicians and the health care system. Anything less would be unfair, unethical. Physicians cannot work miracles. They cannot usher in the utopia which society constantly seeks. Patients, therefore, will need to claim responsibility for their part of the doctor-patient relationship and act more fairly if health care costs are to be equitably contained. This may, in fact, require increased attention to and discussion of what each expects of the other.

The third assumption is: all patients must be treated equitably and with respect for their individual values. This assumption emphasizes the duties of the physician in relation to the patient. This patient focus is necessary because they clearly have the most to win or lose (i.e., their health and life) when they place themselves in the physician's hands. And while they risk their life and health, they are also naive and largely ignorant about the biological, physiological, and pharmacological facts used in medicine. They can be easily misled or manipulated by costly medical advice. This is clearly unethical.

This assumption speaks of equitable treatment and this merits comment because equitable treatment is not equal treatment. Patients can receive equal treatment in such a way as to induce great danger. All diabetics would be treated equally if given the same amount of insulin. But not all diabetics need insulin or the same dosage. An equal dosage in this instance would produce harm.

Equitable treatment is characterized by fairness born of reason: all patients must be treated with reason and in fairness. This concept of "equitability" defies precise definition which would be applicable in all situations and yet it is at the foundation of health care. It is built on the two previous concepts of "well-being" and "respect." The opposite of equitable is arbitrariness, that is, treating individuals by whimsical rules which may change at any moment without ample reason. To treat someone equitably means the responsible exercise of scientific medicine on their behalf and at the same time to respect their values.

The second part of this assumption speaks to the importance of the individual patient's values. These values must be safeguarded because the patient is in a dependent and naive position. Ways to honor these values must be found even when comatose patients are unable to stand up for themselves. Much work remains to be done in this area. The role of the living will in response to extensive use of artificial life support is an example of confusions and struggles with this principle. Indeed, the original impetus of the living will was rooted in efforts to safeguard these individual values and to free the physician from reprisals. Further research is badly needed because it remains unclear whether the living will adequately safeguards these values or physicians.

And yet, individual values must sometimes be challenged. As discussed above, the individual's values must be balanced against society's best interest. When they clearly conflict, some equitable judgment must be made.

Ethical Principles

The preceding discussion has used an ethical perspective to bring a sense of balance to cost containment issues. All parties carry responsibilities for our current cost problems and must participate in the solutions. The three assumptions lay groundwork for preserving what is valuable. These assumptions must now be molded into specific principles relevant to the dilemmas of the cost containment effort. Two brief case studies will provide a context for each ethical principle. Of course, many varied cases could be cited as examples.

CASE STUDIES

Case Study 1

The Triple-A Hospital sought to establish clinics in the community. Its motivation, like that of other hospitals, was to establish an "ambulatory net" in the community which would draw seriously ill or injured patients into its institution. This would supplement admissions from the attending physician staff and increase the occupancy rate.

Triple-A Hospital chose sites for its clinics far to the east of its institution in newly developed suburban areas. Studies showed that these areas possessed inadequate medical care and that the clinics would fill a need.

These plans proceeded smoothly until the hospital Board of Directors reviewed them for approval. Two board members raised serious questions about the plans, noting that the selection of the suburban area seemed motivated not by human need but by administration's assumption that patients from these areas could meet their financial obligations when hospitalized. An intense discussion followed and the plan was finally approved after it was amended to include the placement of clinics in an underserved inner city area.

Principle 1: Providers and payers possess an obligation, even when health care costs are limited, to provide quality care to all sectors of the population.

This is an important statement of principle because, if costs are too high, the natural tendency is to exclude some from the market, to limit availability and/or accessibility. In reality this is a way to limit the sale of health care services and thus reduce the cost.

Such a solution to the cost problem is unethical because it contradicts the first assumption discussed above, i.e., health care must focus on the well-being of individuals and society. The well-being of neither is promoted by excluding some.

Excluding segments of the population from quality health care is unethical because no logical basis exists for making the choice of whom to exclude. Shall we exclude the rich? Perhaps they take care of themselves well and have less need. Shall we exclude males? They seem to use health care less. How about excluding the aged? They have already lived a long life. No convincing logical argument has been made in American health care to exclude any group of individuals. Consequently, exclusion will likely not take place on a logical basis at all, but rather on the basis of who possesses the least power, that is, power to keep themselves included. As demonstrated in the case study, the poor and unemployed are the most likely to be excluded if attention is not given to this principle.

This principle also contradicts another temptation which lurks at every corner. If all must be included in the health care market, then perhaps a lower quality and consequently less costly care can be offered to some persons or geographical locations. Some would be tempted to argue that less quality and cost is needed in working with essentially healthy persons. Some seem tempted to legitimatize less quality and cost in rural, sparsely populated areas. Health care cost, however, cannot be reduced by creating a policy which deliberately delivers lower quality care to selected populations or geographical areas.

Despite this ethical principle and a certain superficial agreement concerning it, analysts point to a two tier medical system which is emerging from the current chaos in health care (Johnson, 1983). Once again two classes of hospital patients are emerging, i.e., private patients and clinic patients. The financing patterns of medicaid and medicare are producing the same distinction in ambulatory care. In such distinctions, the quality of care suffers in part because the financial reimbursement differs. This difference in quality reflects the provider's belief in the maximum that "you get what you pay for." In this instance the quality of what the patient gets is often in proportion to what the doctor (hospital) gets paid. Excessive devotion of physician (or hospital) to this maximum is unethical because it places finances too much at the heart of medical decision making. It loses sight of the assumption that health care delivery must promote the well-being of individuals and society and cannot be governed by economic pragmatism.

Case Study 2

The Triple-A metropolitan area is served by a large competent pediatric hospital which provides over $3 million of uncharged, free service each year. It maintains an emergency room in which the entry charge is $95 and the mean charge per patient visit is $184.

Mr. and Mrs. Jones entered the emergency room with their three children at 8:30 one spring Sunday evening. They were well-known to the staff who noted that no one in the family appeared in distress. At the desk, the mother explained that one child had been wetting the bed at night and now would not go to bed despite her urging. The second child seemed to have a cold; she thought perhaps it was an allergy to grass. When routinely asked if they had talked to their pediatrician or family doctor, the father responded, "No, we just always come here when we want to."

The emergency room physicians found themselves in a familiar dilemma. Did the first child have a bladder infection? Perhaps it was a psychological problem. The second child demonstrated a cough and chest sounds compatible with early pneumonia. The physicians proceeded with complete work-ups for both children because the family had frequently demonstrated that they would not visit a neighborhood pediatrician or family physician. The total charge that evening for the two children was $835.

Principle 2: Society's obligation to provide quality health care is balanced by the duty of the citizens to act responsibly toward such services.

This principle is the counterpart to that described above and entails a number of elements. Each citizen carries the primary responsibility for his/her own health and wellness. As illustrated by the case study, this responsibility implies that citizens must be cognitive of their health care costs even if their insurance covers much of the cost. They also need to provide for routine care, thereby minimizing risks, and provide physicians a fair opportunity to help them at lower costs. This primary responsibility remains with the patient and the family.

In the past, society has willingly borne the cost of health care for patients who have clearly acted irresponsibly. This arrangement meant that society paid when individuals did not take care of their health. Society is, rightfully so, increasingly rejecting this. Employees who smoke receive lesser insurance coverage from the employer's insurance plan or pay higher premiums. In the future, smokers may, in fact, not be eligible for selected, expensive advanced treatment protocols. Similar penalties for health neglective behavior are emerging concerning alcohol intake and seatbelt usage. The ethical viewpoint described here endorses this trend: citizens bear a duty to act responsibly concerning their health.

Society must also use health care services judiciously. Convincing evidence exists that many people experience symptoms but do not see a doctor (White, 1961). These symptoms are usually short-lived and benign. Practitioners are under the impression that 20% of the population use 80% of the services. This percentage includes a group who are chronically ill and whose lives are dependent upon medical care. There are others, however, who have fastened themselves to a physician as a surrogate parent. Their relationship provides them enough support so that they can hold a job or stay out of a hospital. Such working relationships between patient and doctor are admirable, but the current cost containment crisis raises questions as to whether support for such patients can be found elsewhere. Ambulatory care experts agree that between 30-80% of office visits are motivated by significant behavior-emotional concerns. Have not physicians become the father-confessors of the twentieth century? Is there a more economical manner in which to help these patients? Whatever the answer to that question, cost containment efforts must take account of the responsibility invested in both the care-givers and the care-receivers.

Case Study 3

Joan, a waitress and single mother of a three-year-old daughter, began to see a psychiatrist weekly after she became depressed and suicidal. The charge per hour was $120 but the psychiatrist agreed to collect only what her insurance company paid. Joan stabilized during the opening two months of treatment and continued to work on her problems for the next three years although she made very little therapeutic progress. At the end of three years, Joan's insurance company notified her that, in accordance with the policy, they would no longer pay for her psychiatric counseling. They had spent $16,200. Joan promptly terminated treatment, stating that she was unable to pay anything. Four years have passed and Joan has continued to do well.

Principle 3: The relational and reciprocal nature of health care delivery implies that its cost ought to be shared equitably by all.

Two implications of this principle merit discussion. The physician-patient relationship involves many relational and reciprocal concerns. For example, patients who make a physician appointment are obligated to act responsibly and arrive on time (or call to cancel this appointment). The physician is equally obligated not to keep the patient waiting. Or, in another example, patients who seek a physician's opinion are obligated to take it seriously (or to seek a second opinion). Physicians who provide diagnosis and treatment are obligated to do so to the best of their ability. Many other reciprocal obligations are present in the physician-patient relationship, including the obligation of the patient to pay an equitable amount of their cost. Thus this third principle incorporates financial concern into the relational and reciprocal principles developed above. This is justified because the exchange of money for services, whether full cost or fair-share, is a part of the professional relationship.

This patient responsibility cannot be completely passed off to society-in-general who would provide complete payment through taxes. Individual patients perceive such payment as no payment at all; they perceive such care as free and use it accordingly. Yielding to this temptation cannot result in responsible use of health care services.

How can the amount of such a "fair-share" be determined and collected? Such detail is not within the providence of ethics. The point made here is that responsible use of health care will be strengthened by including financial aspects in the actual delivery of services. No magic occurs, of course, if every patient is required to pay something for the physician's visit or the hospital stay. The collected amount will not in itself be substantial, even at a national level. Critics will doubtlessly argue that the amount will be devoured by additional administrative costs. But that is not the point: the patient's financial participation increases the chances of thoughtful decision making by the patient, cutting down on needless use of the system and making it more difficult to use it for surrogate parenting or recreation.

The second implication of this third principle implies that payers and providers must be willing to provide quality care even when the full charge cannot be paid. It implies that the providers and insurance companies must rise above their own perceived "financial need" or arrogant protection of their "standard of living." The inability to cut loose from such a self-protectionistic stance is, from an ethical point of view, not equitable participation in the sharing of health care costs.

Hospitals must also continue to provide quality care when full payment cannot be made. Intense inter-hospital competition will make this difficult. Rivalry between physicians and between hospitals has always existed, but only in the last few years has this rivalry risen above personality conflicts and differences in historical rootage. Only in the last five years, for example, have hometown newspapers run feature articles which compare the cost of hospital rooms and various procedures. Only in the last three years have hospitals begun to advertise themselves to promote their public image so that the patient chooses them over a competitor. This competition may, in fact, lower health care costs.

The emergence of large for-profit corporate structures in health care has raised ethical concerns for many. They fear that these corporations will neglect the needy, leaving the costs of their care to the general public. These developments need to be watched carefully. For-profit corporate structures are not new in health care because most physicians in private practice have traditionally functioned from within their small for-profit corporations, sometimes producing large incomes. Hospitals, on the other hand, are only now moving in this direction and this is not automatically unethical. Large corporate structures may, in fact, be able to construct a more streamlined authority structure and clean out the confusion and waste entrenched at some non-profit institutions. The unanswered question at this time is whether for-profit institutions can satisfactorily protect the well-being of individuals and society. Can they control the lure of more and more profits? Sufficient data are not yet available to answer that question.

As noted at the beginning, these assumptions and ethical principles were developed and discussed as part of the Health Care Cost Containment Public Policy Panel at Ohio State University. They can be applied in many ways since they do not mandate specific policies or programs. This search for applications generated intense discussions among the physicians, nurses, psychologists, social workers, attorneys, and chaplains on the panel. If the principles are taken seriously, such discussions are inevitable because the health care system is being overhauled and no easy solutions exist to the health care cost containment struggle.

What role will chaplains play in this metamorphosis? They can speak to the ethical underpinnings of health care delivery, reminding the medical staff and administration that more than economic welfare is involved as new practice patterns are developed. This role assumes, as is clear from the case examples, that the sole function of chaplains is not to perform pastoral care in a hidden corner of the hospital. Rather, chaplains can speak to the policies and practices of the hospital and its physicians when integrated into the ongoing process of the hospital at the deepest level. In making this contribution, chaplains will have a significant impact on the health care system of the future.

REFERENCES

Abram, M.B., Wolf, S.M. Public Involvement in Medical Ethics. *NEJM*, 1984, *310*, 627-632.

Bayer, R. et al. The Care of Terminally Ill: Morality and Economics. *NEJM*. 1983, *309*, 1490-1494.

Blendon, R.J., Altman, D.E. Public Attitudes About Health Care Cost. *NEJM*. 1984, *311*, 613-616.

Burnham, J. American Medicine's Golden Age: What Happened to It? *Science*, 1982, *215*, 1474-1479.

Culliton, B.J. Medicine as Business: Are Doctors Entrepreneurs? *Science*, 1986, *233*, 1032-1033.

Evans, R.W., Manninen, D.L., Overcast, T.D., Garrison, L.P., Yagi, J., Merrikin, K., Jonsen, A.R. et al. *The National Heart Transplantation Study: Final Report*. Seattle, Washington: Battelle Human Affairs Research Centers, 1984, Vol. 4, Chapters 35-38.

Flexner, A. *Medical Education in the United States and Canada:* A Report to the Carnegie Foundation for the Advancement of Teaching. New York: The Carnegie Foundation, 1910.

Health Care Cost Containment Public Policy Panel of the Commission on Interprofessional Education and Practice. *An Interprofessional Perspective on Health Care Cost Containment*. Ohio State University, 1987.

Huttman, B. A Crime of Compassion. *Newsweek*, August 8, 1983, 15.

Johnson, R.L. Shooting One's Self in the Foot: Congress May Recreate Two-tier Care. *Hospital Progress*, December, 1983, 32-29.

Kapp, M.B. Legal and Ethical Implications of Health Care Reimbursement by Diagnosis Related Group. *Law, Medicine or Health Care*, 1984, 245-253.

Kapp, M.D. Legal and Ethical Standards in Geriatric Medicine. *Journal of the American Geriatrics Society*, 1985, *33*, 179-183.

Marty, Martin. Second Opinion in Health, Faith, Ethics. *Second Opinion*, 1986, *1*: 8-26.

President's Commission on the Health Needs of the Nation. U.S. Government Printing Office, Washington, 1953.

President's Commission for the Study of Ethical Problems in Medicine and Biomedical and Behavioral Research. *Securing Access to Health Care*, 11-47 and 182-197. *Summing Up*, 65-76. U.S. Government Printing Office, Washington D.C., March, 1983.

Wanzer, S.H. et al. The Physician's Responsibility Toward Hopelessly Ill Patients. *NEJM*, 1984, *310*, 955-959.

White, K.L., Williams, F., Greenberg, B. Ecology of Medical Care. *NEJM*, 1961, *265*:885-892.

Issues in Long Term Care

Daniel G. Kratz, MA

SUMMARY. Chaplaincy in a long term care facility requires attention to specialized concerns related to the extended length of stay. This article argues the need to (1) retain or restore resident's home church tie; (2) be sensitive to resident/family communications; (3) participate in an interdisciplinary team; (4) understand when to maintain confidentiality and when to speak; (5) know who needs spiritual nourishment.

INTRODUCTION

The church has historically been an innovator in the field of health care. The first hospitals were sponsored by churches and religious orders. Similarly, the concept of a long term care facility as we know it today has its roots in what were once "Church Homes."

The church, in starting these institutions, assumed that their very nature as a "religious" setting made pastoral care easy. This has two consequences for our consideration. First, we find that many long term care facilities, not only under church auspices, but also in the private sector today, have an administrator with ordination and/or a background in ministry. Secondly, it has often been assumed that no special training is necessary for the pastoral care giver in the long term setting (variously called Chaplain or sometimes simply "pastor").

Daniel G. Kratz, Director of Chaplains, Manor HealthCare, RD #2 Box 850, Schuylkill Haven, PA 17972.

The cases in this article have been altered to protect identity. Some cases may be a composite of more than one resident.

More recently we have seen some movement towards the calling of well-trained persons to the field of long term care Chaplain, but the structure and nature of the position, as well as standard of competency are still in their infancy.

It is our position that the long term care setting requires skills and training at least comparable with those of the Hospital Chaplain, that careful planning needs to be devoted to the type of ministry to be rendered and that intentionality and accountability are needed to ensure that the skills and efforts expended are congruent with the ministry that is needed.

We do not expect to provide a comprehensive view of the entire job of a long term care Chaplain, but rather to highlight a few of the important issues. A selection of case studies will illustrate these points for our consideration.

I. THE LONG TERM CARE CHAPLAIN MUST SEEK TO RETAIN/RESTORE THE RESIDENT'S HOME CHURCH TIE

Many long term care residents are searching for a sense of meaning to their lives. There is often a pervasive sense of loss — loss of spouse, loss of the homestead, loss of friends, loss of vigor, loss of independence are some of the very real experiences of the average resident.

JQ was an 82-year-old widower, admitted to a long term care facility with a diagnosis of cerebral atrophy. He was still physically able, and often alert and lucid, though with some "forgetful" spells. His family consisted of one daughter and a son-in-law. There was no extended family and no grandchildren.

Prior to entry to the nursing center, JQ had lived with his daughter and son-in-law for 18 years, following the death of his wife. While the daughter was sincerely concerned about her father, family circumstances made it impossible for her to visit more than weekly.

JQ had been a carpenter by trade and readily took to the Arts and Crafts program. He was pleasant and friendly, but felt a sense of loneliness. Upon admission, JQ stated that he was "an *INACTIVE* Catholic!!" (emphasis his.) He readily made friends with the Chaplain and attended Bible Story Time and the Sunday Ecumenical Workship services.

The Chaplain spent time in getting acquainted and reminiscing with the hopes of discovering what might be the cause of the evident hostility to his church in his statement upon admission.

It gradually emerged that JQ had been married at the age of 15. His wife "ran off" six months later and was never heard from again. JQ obtained a divorce and later was happily married for nearly 40 years prior to the death of his wife.

He had accepted excommunication as his lot, and had never sought annulment of his first marriage or restoration to membership in the Roman Catholic Church. He nevertheless raised his daughter as a faithful adherent and identified himself as "Catholic" (albeit INACTIVE!). He was of the opinion that the Catholic Church would require that he confess to a sin in getting a divorce and stated that he did not believe he had sinned and would "never" go to confession.

The Chaplain consulted with the local Roman Catholic pastor and Bishop, who agreed that in light of his more than 50 years of faithful living he need not go through a confession about his divorce at a tender age. A written pardon was secured to satisfy his question whether this was really true, and the local pastor pronounced absolution.

JQ began attending weekly Mass at the facility, and soon made friends with a Catholic layman who picked him up and took him to weekly Mass at the Church as well.

It would have been easy for the Chaplain to encourage JQ in seeing himself as a "member" of the congregation at the nursing center. This is especially true in the long-term care setting as contrasted to the hospital, because of the more "permanent" nature of the placement. To do so, however, would deny the full sense of belonging which could be obtained by restoring him to his home church, from which he had been long estranged. JQ did, in fact, not only enjoy his home church once more, but established a new group of friends in addition to the friends and congregants in the center.

This would not occur without the intentionality of maintaining the home church tie. The Chaplain ought not become the resident's pastor.

II. THE LONG TERM CARE CHAPLAIN MUST BE SENSITIVE TO COMMUNICATIONS AND THE DYNAMICS OF EACH INDIVIDUAL RESIDENT AND FAMILY SYSTEM

There are many occasions when the elder person, with some progressive dementia, is perceived as not fully knowing what is happening to and around him/her. There are many occasions when the same story is repeated or when similar stories are heard for what seems like the thousandth time.

Solid training, and awareness of our own "baggage" and sensitive listening are essential. We cannot afford the luxury of pigeon-holes or assumptions.

RP was a terminal patient in her upper eighties. She had entered the nursing center when her cancer reached the point that she could no longer be self sustaining at home. She had no family. Her financial affairs were attended by a bank trust officer. Her only visitor was her pastor, who stopped in twice a month, and one neighbor who occasionally came to see her. There was little that could be done for her, except to provide comfort for her last days.

When she first entered the center, she was able to sit up in a chair and visited in a pleasant and friendly manner with the staff and the Chaplain. She had been a very active church member and spoke warmly about her faith and enthusiastically about her religious upbringing and her church experiences.

As she began to fail, she became bedfast, and it was soon : evident that the end was now near. She began to be fearful and apprehensive.

All attempts at comfort were to no avail. In fact, the nursing staff said that she seemed to be more agitated and fearful after visits from her pastor and the Chaplain.

The Chaplain took this information seriously and visited to

learn why this might be. As often before, RP talked freely about her home and church. She stated with emphasis, "My father *was* a good man!" The Chaplain noted the defensive tone and facilitated further expression about her father's goodness. It gradually emerged that RP was saying, "Although he used to beat my mother and sometimes beat me also, Daddy went to church and prayed, so he must have been good. Besides, in spite of everything I loved him."

Further conversation revealed a deep sense of fear about "Meeting Daddy again" (Will he still be punishing and angry?) and about "Meeting God" (Is "Our Father in Heaven" as brutal as my Father on earth?). Subsequent interpretation of her feelings was of some help. Though the time was too short to resolve this long-seated fear and trauma.

When her pastor and the Chaplain avoided the picture of God as Father, and focused on the Good Shepherd who loves and cares for his sheep, RP was able to receive the comfort of her faith.

This long-hidden family problem would never have surfaced, without the careful attention which the Chaplain paid first to the staff who observed the sudden change in reaction to RP's religious visitors and then to the little revealing nuance of tone in the conversation of RP herself.

III. THE LONG TERM CARE CHAPLAIN MUST BE PART OF THE INTERDISCIPLINARY TEAM

When the Chaplain is seen as a "lone ranger" or when the Chaplain sees himself as the only spiritual caregiver, or when pastoral care is seen as a "tacked on" extra, the full healing potential of spiritual care is not possible. Real healing requires accurate diagnosis so that treatment can be effective.

GJ, a 92-year-old gentleman with congestive heart failure, was admitted to the long term care facility, since his family was no longer able to care for him. His wife of 52 years was frail, and his three children were all in their late 60s and not able to help. GJ needed help with dressing, bathing and walking, but was able to sit comfortably in an easy chair and take part in light activities so long as he was watched and help was readily available when he felt weak or short of breath. His family was attentive, and scarcely a day went by without a visit from one of them.

GJ was always pleased to visit with the Chaplain, and attended almost all religious activities, though he did not attempt to take an active part in either discussion or singing, because of his shortness of breath. Other staff members were somewhat concerned about GJ and felt that he was not really feeling very well at all.

In the Interdisciplinary Care Planning meeting some months after GJ's admission, one of the nurses mentioned that GJ was very "depressed." Other staff members agreed, with the exception of the Chaplain and the social worker, both of whom had not seen evidence of depression. The nurse's conclusion was based on her observation that "GJ often says he wants to die." Neither the Chaplain or the social worker had ever heard this from GJ.

In subsequent visits the Chaplain attempted to address the question, but was not successful in eliciting any opening in the direction of either depression or "death wishes." Finally she ventured to say to GJ, "The nurse said that you told her you wanted to die." GJ blushed, and said, "I didn't really mean it." "But," said the Chaplain, "you said it more than once." To which GJ replied, "I like the way they fuss over me when they think I'm upset."

The joint efforts of the nurse, activities staff, social worker and Chaplain were able to help GJ learn to enjoy more constructive and positive interaction in the days that followed. His innate shyness and awe in the "medical" setting were the cause of his adopting this manipulative style—but he carefully shielded it from those whom he knew would address it. Team analysis and treatment were essential to a constructive solution.

IV. THE LONG TERM CARE CHAPLAIN MUST BE SENSITIVE TO ISSUES OF CONFIDENTIALITY, KNOWING AND TELLING

The Chaplain in a long term care facility will be confronted with many situations involving ethics of confidentiality and wisdom. The staff in long term care are particularly susceptible to "burn-out." The residents they know best and come to love and care for very deeply are precisely the ones who have been in the facility the longest and are gradually failing and dying—with no physical heal-ing for us to offer them. The family of the cancer victim may be concerned about who should or shouldn't be told. The ethics of withdrawal of treatment are daily emotional drains to staff and fam-ily alike. In all this the Chaplain is expected to act with sensitivity and wisdom.

> ML was admitted to the long term care facility with terminal lung cancer. She was in her early eighties, a widow, with one son. Her son visited regularly. She had a persistent cough, and increasing weakness and congestion. From time to time as her condition worsened she would visit the hospital for tests or treatment, always returning within a very few days. She was comfortable in the nursing center, and stated that she was glad to "get back home" when she returned to the center. She stated that she didn't know why she went to the hospital any-way, since it wasn't helping much.
>
> Her physician had written "Do not notify patient of diagno-sis" on her chart because "he and the family felt she could not take the news."
>
> ML frequently asked the nurses "What's really wrong with me?" In visits with the Chaplain she said she wished the doc-tor would tell her more. This was relayed to the doctor, but neither the son nor the doctor was willing to discuss the situa-tion with respect to the diagnosis.
>
> After some time, ML stated to the Chaplain, "I think the

doctor's lying." The Chaplain asked why. She replied, "He says I'm doing well and I can tell I'm getting worse." The Chaplain asked what she thought about that. She said, "I think I have lung cancer. I'm not afraid to say it, I just wish somebody would talk about it." The Chaplain did, and felt that a sense of satisfaction was reached by the resident.

The doctor was notified of the conversation. At his next visit he alluded to the Chaplain's conversation but did not directly discuss the diagnosis. When the Chaplain visited later that day, ML said "Dr. Z was in, and guess what!" "What?" "He's more afraid than I am. His mother was a friend of mine, and she had cancer too. He won't admit it, but he just can't bring himself to talk about it, because I remind him of her."

In later weeks the Chaplain was able to give pastoral care to the physician for his unresolved feelings of grief and helplessness.

These conflicts of loyalties are even sharper when the person in need of counseling is a member of the staff.

BD was a nursing assistant who was in a difficult marital situation. She came to the Chaplain for counseling. It gradually emerged that she was being abused by her husband. One day she stated, "Sometimes I get like him. I can't control myself. When L (her nine-year-old daughter) does something I just hit her without thinking."

The Chaplain could immediately foresee the possibility of resident abuse, should this acting out happen at work. Clearly, confidentiality is owed to the counselee while security is owed to the residents.

The Chaplain pointed out the possibility of losing her temper with a resident and asked if BD was willing to talk to her supervisor. She was not. The Chaplain then asked for permission to talk to the supervisor on BD's behalf. This permission was given and it was possible to transfer her to an area where she did not have direct patient contact until her personal problems were resolved.

It should be noted that had permission to consult with the

supervisor been denied the Chaplain would have been forced to discuss the limits of confidentiality with a view to protecting resident safety even at the expense of the trust of this particular employee.

V. THE LONG TERM CARE CHAPLAIN MUST BRING SPIRITUAL RESOURCES TO THOSE WHO NEED NOURISHMENT

Our openness and non-directive approach, our tolerance and ecumenicity, our acceptance and listening skills must not be allowed to become so all-encompassing that we have no resources to give to those who need religious guidance.

SS was an elderly widow, who had been admitted to the nursing center due to advanced arthritis, and increasing weakness due to many minor problems. She was a large woman, and now that she was bedfast her family could no longer care for her.

SS often expressed a sense of weariness and longing to join her husband in heaven. One day when talking to the Chaplain she said, "Chaplain, I'm 96 years old. Everyone who went to the Township School with me is gone — even the ones who were in first grade when I was in eighth. My husband has been dead for 19 years. We had seven children, five of them are dead, and Jim and Mary aren't in very good health either — wouldn't surprise me if they go soon. Even two of my grandchildren have died. Now, Chaplain, I've always tried to live a good life, why doesn't God want me? I'm tired and want to go home to Him."

To the questions about meaning of life, the penetrating puzzle of "why good people suffer" the Chaplain must bring a sound theological viewpoint and a willingness not only to explore feelings but also to contribute resources.

The sacrament of communion, with its appeal to the sense of smell, taste and vision as well as the repetition of the old familiar words is often the only recognizable event in the life of one with cerebral deterioration. The use of familiar hymns and prayers, the offering of advice and comfort, the healing touch, the pardon given when confession has been heard and the pain of guilt not only expressed but explored and experienced — these are resources that the sensitive Chaplain must be willing to use.

There is a time when it is not an act of kindness to demand that the resident must not only have a need and feel it, but also be willing to *ask* for the help that is needed. The long term care resident often needs more structure, more guidance and more help than many are willing to offer.

CONCLUSION

A well-trained, caring and sensitive Chaplain can make a major difference in the long term care facility. Healing can be fostered both physically and spiritually. Peace of mind and comfort can be given. Staff can be helped to have sharper insight and more effective interactions.

We have tried to demonstrate just a few of the key principles that we need to keep in mind as we approach ministry in the long term care setting: (1) The long term care Chaplain must seek to retain/restore the resident's home church tie, (2) The long term care Chaplain must be sensitive to communications and the dynamics of each individual resident and family system, (3) The long term care Chaplain must be part of the interdisciplinary team, (4) The long term care Chaplain must be sensitive to issues of confidentiality, knowing, and telling, (5) The long term care Chaplain must bring spiritual resources to those who need nourishment.

Caring for Those Who Wait:
The Chaplain's Role as a Member of a Multidisciplinary Surgical Team

Robert D. Craig

Traditionally, pastoral care in the hospital for surgical patients and their families is limited. Restricted access to the pre-operative, surgical and recovery room areas usually confines the chaplain's ministry to the patient's room, the waiting room, and perhaps the surgical intensive care unit.

From our own experiences as chaplains for an open heart surgical team, we are keenly aware of the anxiety which prevails in the surgical waiting room. Research cited in the professional nursing journal, *Surgical Rounds*, confirmed our perceptions that "families experience considerable anxiety, alterations in time perceptions, and feelings of isolation from the health care team" (Silva, 1978). Building upon our well-established role as open heart chaplains, we wanted to provide some measure of pastoral care for patients and their families in general surgery (Johnson & Kerk, 1981).

Increasingly, families of patients having other kinds of surgery would ask us to obtain information for them when they heard us providing detailed accounts of open heart surgeries. The only contact families had with surgery was through a Volunteer Surgical Hostess who telephoned the appropriate waiting room after the patient arrived in the Recovery Room. After 3:30 p.m. and on weekends, there was no source of communication. We assumed this was a common dilemma for waiting families in hopitals. An article in *Today's OR Nurse* indicates that based upon their research, "during

---

Robert D. Craig is affiliated with the Methodist Medical Center, Peoria, IL.

© 1988 by The Haworth Press, Inc. All rights reserved.

31

the time the patient was in the operating room, spouses reported little or no meaningful communication with members of the health care team" (Silva, 1984). As chaplains, we felt that our role should be and could be expanded to include these waiting families. This meant establishing relationships with an entirely different staff of nurses and surgeons. New ways of obtaining surgical information were needed. The actual surgical reporting would be different. We had no established referral source of surgical patients.

We began by meeting with the Clinical Coordinators for the Surgical Preparation Area, Surgery, and the Recovery Room and indicated our wish to work with them in conveying information to waiting families. They shared our concern and were eager to cooperate. Before implementing this new program we familiarized ourselves with protocol in general surgery:

- One hour prior to the scheduled surgery "start time" the patient is brought to a Surgical Preparation Area (SPA).
- Usually about one half hour in the operating room elapses with the induction of anesthesia and "prepping" before the incision is made.
- Unless the patient is to be admitted directly to the Surgical Intensive Care Unit from surgery, they spend one hour in the Recovery Room before returning to their room.

During our coverage of surgery we change into surgical "greens." To maintain sterile conditions in the operating room, a paper, disposable coverall is worn over the surgical greens and surgical cap, mask, and shoe covers are changed prior to re-entry into the surgical area.

While we enjoy excellent rapport with the cardiovascular surgeons, we knew we could not expect a similar reception from all the surgeons in general surgery. Clearly, some surgeons see the chaplain as an unwelcome intruder on their "turf." Information cannot always be obtained by entering the operating room. For this reason, a communication network consisting of operating room nurses, ward clerks, and Surgical Preparation Area and Recovery Room nurses was devised so that the Chaplain could obtain information on all surgeries.

To build rapport with the OR nurses, we conducted an inservice seminar. We explained the rationale for surgical reporting, but most importantly, let the nurses know how we used or conveyed surgical information to families. A time for their own questions was also provided.

While our reporting for open heart surgery is very detailed, we knew we could not accurately report on general surgeries with the same detail. Conveying the sequence of events in surgery enables families to cope with their waiting much easier. Periodic reports from surgery dissipates families' anxieties because they are not left waiting and wondering. These frequent reports modify a family's stress so they are better able to "hear" and understand what the surgeon reports to them following surgery. Therefore, our reports consist of: the time the patient is moved from the SPA to the OR, when the patient is asleep, when the incision is made, the "close," and the patient's transfer to the Recovery Room.

Each day a copy of the surgical schedule is routed to our office. The schedule lists patient name, room number, surgery time, surgeon name, and procedure. The surgical schedule serves a dual purpose. First, it helps us to identify surgical procedures which could be more anxiety-producing, either by the length of time in surgery (a radical neck dissection lasting 6-8 hours); or by the diagnostic nature of the surgery (a breast biopsy with possible radical mastectomy). Secondly, the schedule helps us to identify the units where the majority of surgical patients come from.

We make regular (once every hour) rounds to these waiting rooms to inquire who is waiting for patients in surgery. We do not identify ourselves as chaplains until after we have briefly explained the service we can provide as a liaison between the family and the surgical area. In this way, the family's stress is not magnified with the chaplain's presence.

Some surgeons have grown to trust us and communicate with us routinely. Words of appreciation have filtered back to them from patients' families who were kept informed during surgery. We have come to know some of the surgeons on a more personal basis over coffee and casual conversations in the surgeon's lounge. Our time spent in the lounge is very intentional for building relationships and maintaining our "visibility" as a member of the surgical team. An orthopedic surgeon requested that we routinely follow and report on all the Harrington Rod surgeries he does. Within the past year, other surgeons have come to routinely expect that we will report on their surgeries.

As word of this new surgical liaison service spread through the Medical Center, other referral sources developed. Unit chaplains learn of patients scheduled for surgery in report and refer to the surgical chaplain. Nurses in the SPA refer patients who are usually apprehensive. When a patient's surgery is delayed, the surgical chaplain is notified so families can be made aware of the delay. Occasionally, the Surgical Hostess encounters an anxious family member who calls repeatedly. When this happens the chaplain is notified and establishes contact with the family.

Of course, not all surgeries can be successful or achieve the hoped-for results. When unexpected problems arise or a death occurs in the operating room the ministry of the surgical chaplain takes on even greater significance. The "bad news" does not come totally unexpectedly to the family. Through reports by the chaplain, families learn of the realities in surgery as they develop. In this way, families are better prepared for the possibility of the patient's death.

CASE STUDY

Mary W. was a 64-year-old patient admitted to our hospital after repeated hospitalizations at another hospital. She lived with her husband, John, who is retired. They have two grown sons. John and Mary recently joined the United Methodist Church. Mary was approximately 5'2" and weighed 200 pounds. She was diabetic and had had one kidney removed. Mary contended all through her hospitalization that her shortness of breath and weakness was due to her diabetes. Her husband, John, reinforced that belief and tended to be very protective of Mary, fearing any news other than what Mary wanted to hear would "upset her too much."

I met Mary the day after she was admitted to our hospital. From our first meeting, Mary seemed extremely frightened. She reminded me of a wide-eyed, frightened animal almost paralyzed with fear. Mary "hid" under blankets while in bed and even sitting in the chair. It was work to engage Mary in conversation as she offered minimal verbal responses. (Later, her pastor indicated that he had experienced her this way during previous hospitalizations.) The conversations were mainly with John, who rarely left Mary's bedside.

After Mary failed the treadmill test, she had an angiogram which showed severe coronary artery disease. Surgery was suggested, which Mary at first refused. After further discussion with her doctor and John, she reluctantly relented and was scheduled for surgery on a Monday. Janet, Mary's nurse, remarked to me how difficult it was to do the pre-op teaching, and that Mary refused to see the Intensive Care Unit. "Open Heart" patients are shown the Intensive Care Unit where they will be post-op. She asked me to try to impress upon Mary the importance of attitude in going through open heart surgery. In a conversation in the hall with John, I mentioned Mary's fright and depression, and John indicated when she had been "this way" before, their pastor had been able to talk with Mary and help her. I called their pastor, and he agreed to come to see Mary, which he did. The day of surgery, I learned Mary had been cancelled because she had a fever. At one point, the surgeons were considering sending Mary home to recuperate and then return for surgery. John protested and Mary stayed in the hospital until the next week when she had her surgery. I talked with Mary the day before the surgery.

Before the nurse took Mary into the Operating Room, she remarked to me, "That lady is scared to death." The surgeons did three bypasses. It became necessary to insert the intra-aortic balloon pump to sustain Mary's heart after she came off the heart-lung machine. During the course of the surgery, I informed John about Mary's progress. I felt that as I told John of the progress he was more optimistic than realistic and that he had failed to weigh the additional risk factors (i.e., diabetes, loss of one kidney, hypertension, and Mary's weight). Even as I tried to temper John's optimism (the time after surgery in ICU is still critical) he seemed not to hear that. Mary's surgery was longer than usual. Afterward, John breathed a sigh of relief that the surgery was over, and I encouraged him to go to the cafeteria for a break, which he did. Even though I was not aware of any clinical problems occurring during surgery, I did not breathe a sigh of relief. I did not feel as optimistic about this as I had about others.

I followed the second surgery for the day through, then checked to see if John had gotten in to see Mary yet. He had not because Mary's blood pressure was not stabilizing, and she did not have any pulse in either of her legs. The nurse felt we would have to go back to surgery to try to restore the pulses. She said she had never seen anything like it before. Mary's legs were cold, blue and stiff, as if rigor mortis had already set in Mary's legs. The nurse asked me if the family was in the waiting room. I had just sent them to the cafeteria for supper, so I went to get John.

John saw me coming into the cafeteria, got up from the table and rushed toward me.

J: What's wrong, Bob? Is anything wrong? Is Mary OK?
C: John, she may have to go back for more surgery. When you're finished with supper, the doctor would like to talk with you.
J: What's wrong, is it her heart?
C: No, right now her heart is fine. As I understand it, she's having some circulation problems in her legs, and they need to find out why. The surgeon can give you more details. You will have to sign another permit for surgery though. (John turns to his sister.)
J: I was afraid of this. We've got to call my sons right away.

We went back down to the waiting room. The doctor came out to talk with John and explained that they wanted to take Mary back to surgery as soon as they had finished with the second surgery. John made his phone calls in one of the offices adjacent to the SICU waiting room. As soon as his son answered, John broke down and couldn't talk. His sister explained the situation. John returned to the waiting room, and I let him know when Mary went back to surgery. Mary had not really awakened from the anesthetic of her first surgery yet. John's greatest fear then was that Mary would have to be "opened up" again (have her chest opened again) and go on the heart-lung machine. I indicated to him that that would not be necessary if they just did surgery on her legs.

Mary's second surgery lasted until approximately 2:30 a.m. the next morning, when she died.

I remained with John until the conclusion of the surgery, bringing him periodic surgical reports. Arrangements were made for John to see Mary after her death prior to his leaving the hospital. I attended Mary's visitation at the funeral home and spoke further with John and his sons.

This ministry is valuable not only for families, but also for the surgeons. Being physically and emotionally fatigued, it understandably is difficult for a surgeon to confront an anxious, waiting family with "bad news." The chaplain can be an emotional "buffer" for the surgeon and process some of the grief reactions expressed by the family when a surgery does not conclude as hoped. Significant "bonding" between chaplain and family frequently occurs during the operative period. This "bonding" enables the chaplain to establish a relationship with a family for further pastoral care and support.

Two designated surgical chaplains work alternating days in surgery. Late surgeries and emergencies raised the potential for our own "burnout" because we maintain 24 hour, 7 days a week on call coverage for the open heart team as well. In order to provide after hours surgical coverage, we utilize our CPE students. As on call chaplain, they can report on late surgeries or emergencies until their conclusion. A telephone communication system with the office in surgery was established. This eliminates the need for the on call chaplain to change into "greens." All CPE students take part in a seminar taught by one of the surgical chaplains.

Instruments for documenting our pastoral care to surgical patients were devised. We keep a daily surgical log indicating surgical procedure, referral source, surgeon, chaplain, and the patient's name. Copies of each week's log are forwarded to the Director of our Pastoral Care Department and periodically to the hospital administrator. A report is compiled at the end of each year indicating the number of surgeries followed, the type followed (cardiovascular or general), and percentage increases or decreases in comparison with the previous year. Over 2,700 surgical procedures were reported on in 1984.

Let me conclude by briefly addressing our underlying philosophy for this unique style of pastoral care. The role of servant as defined by ministry implies service rendered in the name of Christ. It is our belief that such service is limited only by the boundaries of our own human creativity. Concluding remarks in the article mentioned earlier from *Today's OR Nurse* state, "health care personnel have a professional responsibility to assist spouses and other family members cope with the surgical experience in a positive way" (Silva, 1984). Developing the surgical liaison program enables us to respond to patients and families in not only a professional way, but a pastoral way as well.

This extension of pastoral care to previously "forgotten" patients and their families has more thoroughly integrated our ministry into the structure of Methodist Medical Center. We now interact routinely with all levels of health care team. With this multidisciplinary team concept, Methodist Medical Center is able to provide more comprehensive health care. Furthermore, the delivery of that health care through surgical intervention is truly comprehensive, meeting the physical, spiritual, and emotional needs of the patient and the patient's family for further pastoral care and support.

THE TEN COMMANDMENTS OF SURGICAL REPORTING

1. Respect the individual preferences and personalities of each surgeon. Never enter a surgical suite without some kind of agreement or understanding.
2. Do not deny families information because it is difficult to obtain information. Use the surgical personnel to secure information.
3. Always clarify with the surgeon what information he wants you to disclose to the family, i.e., a newly confirmed malignancy.
4. Walk slowly with bad news. Only report anxiety producing information when you are able to put it into proper perspective or you absolutely have no other choice.
5. Always follow through in your reporting. Don't promise what you can't or are unwilling to deliver. Expectations not

fulfilled create their own anxieties. If you begin reporting on a surgery, follow through until the patient arrives in the Recovery Room.

6. Observe proper sterile techniques. Entry to surgical areas is made wearing surgical "greens." Appropriate changes of surgical cap, shoe covers, and mask should be adhered to.

7. Be sensitive to emotionally charged situations. Even the most cooperative nurses and surgeons may find themselves in the midst of an emergency or difficult procedure and be unable to provide you with information. Common courtesy dictates that the chaplain wait until personnel are free to answer questions or that you seek out other personnel for information.

8. Desensitize the presence of the chaplain in the waiting room as soon as possible. State how you can be of service to families before introducing yourself as a surgical chaplain.

9. Do nothing to violate the confidence a patient and family have in their physician. Never allow your own personal feelings about physicians to contaminate the physician-patient-family relationships.

10. Check and recheck. Always correctly identify waiting family members. As the chaplain makes rounds to several waiting rooms and to several family members there is an increasing margin for error.

BIBLIOGRAPHY

Johnson, Howard and Larry Kirk. "Building the Chaplain's Role on the Comprehensive Cardiovascular Care Team." *American Protestant Hospital Association Bulletin*, 1981.

Silva, Mary. "Caring for Those Who Wait." *Today's OR Nurse*, 1984.

Silva, Mary. "Effects of Orientation on Spouses' Anxieties toward Hospitalization and Surgery." *Res. Nurse and Health*, 1979.

Silva, Mary. "How the Patient's Spouse Views the Operation." *Surgical Rounds*, 1978.

Decision-Making in the Seriously Ill: Facing Possibility and Limitation

Richard J. Gerber, MEd, MDiv, MTh

SUMMARY. This article discusses the nature of and role of psychological/spiritual maturity in the decision-making of the seriously ill. The author presents a four-spoked continuum designed to portray decisional struggles that he has observed in seriously ill persons. Such decision-making largely seems to be a function of one entertaining "possibility" but acting out of "limitation."

Life can only be understood backwards; but it must be lived forwards.[1]

Sören Kierkegaard

As a hospital chaplain who has ministered to seriously ill persons and their families over the last fifteen years, I have developed some definite impressions related to how such persons approach decision-making when struggling with their diseases. Knowledge about how one makes decisions when under the stress of serious illness can be important on various levels. For the ill person such knowledge can provide some objectivity, power, security and control in a very subjective, impotent, frightening and ambiguous process. In short, it can bring the seriously ill person more clarity and peace in a poten-

Richard J. Gerber is Director of Clinical Pastoral Education, Mercy Medical Center, 4050 Coon Rapids Boulevard, Coon Rapids, MN 55433-2586.

tially ego-shattering experience. As a 51-year-old man who was dying of pancreatic cancer once said in a cancer support group I co-led, "I'm scared as hell about dying and dealing with all that lies ahead, but it sure helps to hear other people's experiences so you at least know a little about what to expect." For family members, friends and professional helpers, understanding the processes and needs of the seriously ill discourages unhelpful projection of one's own fears and needs onto these persons thus freeing one to be more effective in offering creative support. Such seemed to be the case for one of my clinical pastoral education students when a 66-year-old hospice patient told her: "I really feel listened to and accepted by you. You're not just full of advice like my family and many of my friends." This article, then, is for those who are ill but also for those who are healthy. It is especially for those who intimately feel and embrace these two realities as but opposite sides of the same coin . . . their coin.

MATURITY, STRESS AND DECISION-MAKING

In *The Denial of Death*, Ernest Becker states, "If there is tragic limitation in life there is also possibility. What we call maturity is the ability to see the two in some kind of balance into which we can fit creatively."[2] In other terms, maturity has to do with the relative balance between (1) openness to an unlimited reality which is always beyond our ability to experience and/or understand completely and (2) our tendency to constrict or partialize reality into manageable and understandable categories. Mature persons embrace both "possibility" and "limitation" within themselves, accept ambiguity as the inescapable context of life, and struggle to live their unique pilgrimages as important contributions that broaden the web of existence. Such was the case with Ms. Shatner. She was a 48-year-old woman struggling with the end stages of breast cancer. She talked openly with her family about dying and about how much she would miss them, but she also shared how much she valued every day and each experience with them as they battled the disease together. She felt God, too, was in the battle with her giving her strength, guidance and courage. When she did die, her children spoke of her great legacy to them: "Mom taught us how to look pain and hardship in the eye while focusing our energy where it could do the most good — in the shared experiences of the seemingly little things of everyday life."

Immature persons, on the other hand, generally deny or repress too severely either "possibility" or "limitation." They often seem psychologically and spiritually single faceted and rigid. Extreme forms of such immaturity can cause persons to appear as rampant idealists, dogmatic activists or passive cowards. For example, Mr. Smith, a 52-year-old heart patient, refused to accept his physical limitations because he believed God would determine his fate. This rampant idealistic attitude resulted in Mr. Smith's not slowing down his workaholic pace. He exacerbated his heart condition to the point of his total disability within one year after its initial diagnosis. Somewhat similarly, 38-year-old Ms. Herald, upon being told she had Hodgkin's disease, dogmatically refused any treatment — labeling it as "unnatural." Though the odds were that the treatment would prolong her life with quite decent physical quality, she nonetheless literally packed her bags and headed across country declaring to see as much of life as possible before "checking out." Then there are those who respond like 42-year-old Ms. Johnson. Looking like a passive coward, she refused to accept any responsibility for deciding whether or not to undergo chemotherapy once she was diagnosed as having leukemia. She finally did agree to the treatment after considerable prodding by both family and physician, but she tearfully underwent each therapy cycle stating her confusion about whether or not she should continue. Regarding God, she stated: "He just sits up in His heaven and watches me suffer down here."

The stress of serious illness often momentarily alters one's usual sense of maturity. It may "knock one off his or her pins" for a time requiring patience, struggle and acceptance to regain equilibrium. Such stress may result in one's permanently decompensating or in moving one toward a deeper sense of maturity than experienced before the onset of the illness. Genuine caring and professional counseling can help seriously ill persons mature. Such seemed to be the case with the 66-year-old hospice patient ministered to by the clinical pastoral education student mentioned earlier.

In short, decision-making in the seriously ill largely seems to be a function of entertaining "possibility" but acting out of "limitation." Seriously ill persons seem to struggle to apply the following general process to their very specific situations. Making decisions means they must close off options, define a situation in a particular way and accept the consequences of their actions. The more persons can do this deliberately and firmly but without claiming absolute, universal "rightness" for their decisions, the more they are solidly grounded in their creatureliness (claiming their humble commonness with all of struggling humanity). Failure to do this results in their living as if they know more than is the case. Such persons adopt a god-like posture and they define themselves primarily over and against much of struggling humanity. Persons who claim such absolute, universal "rightness" for their decisions can do so either consciously or unconsciously; and they can seem either weak or strong. On one extreme, they may appear to be confident, self-contained "islands" in a sea of uncertainty; or on the other extreme, they may seem like immature children almost totally dependent on the will of others to define their existence. Such "immature children" at first glance appear to be anything but god-like; but, subtly, they act as though they know exactly how they fit into the world (knowledge available only to an omniscient deity). They have singularly determined that it is primarily up to others to ameliorate their pain and/or invite their health and wholeness. What is missing for both the "self-contained islands" and the "immature children" is a creative sense of peership or mutuality in which they feel to be both embedded in community as well as a unique defining force in its ongoing development.

DYNAMICS IN DECISION-MAKING: A FOUR-SPOKED CONTINUUM

As indicated earlier, serious illness upsets one's equilibrium and places him or her in a new reality. In struggling to discover possibilities and act out of limitations, numerous dynamics come into play. Following is a four-spoked continuum designed to portray decisional struggles that I have observed in seriously ill persons. These are but four foci on what I suspect could be a continuum with numerous spokes or dynamics. Hopefully this selected limited paradigm will point some direction and aid in our understanding of decision-making with the seriously ill. (See Figure 1.)

Let us briefly discuss each of these spokes or dynamics. Regarding the Isolated/Open spoke, it would seem that seriously ill persons vary in their desire to involve others in making important decisions. Some tend to shut others out often under the guise of helping or protecting them. However, often belying such isolated, arbitrary action is something akin to what Freud described as the intrapsychic struggle between the pleasure principle and the reality principle.[3] The pleasure principle is that part of us that looks for instant gratification. When pain or discomfort is felt, impulsively we seek to avoid it and flee to a more pleasurable state. The conditions of others are important to us only insofar as they satisfy our impatient need to get what we want. In this regard, the more one is bound to the pleasure principle (as seemed to be the case with Ms. Johnson mentioned earlier), the more one isolates him or herself from the contributions of others that may challenge, stimulate change and invite a level of living which includes a broader perspective on real-

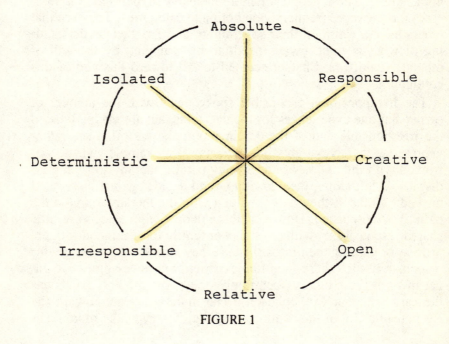

FIGURE 1

ity. Freud's reality principle, on the other hand, encourages us to be more measured and less impulsive. It invites us toward openness, to tolerate greater degrees of tension so that options can be considered and a variety of behavior chosen. Others are valued and needed because they offer differing perspectives which broaden our reality base thus enabling us to direct our lives more inclusively while allowing for greater degrees of ambiguity. Ms. Shatner seemed to embody much toward the "open" end of this continuum spoke.

The Absolute/Relative spoke has to do with how seriously ill persons value the sovereignty of their lives. The more they are located toward the absolute end of the continuum the more they see their "right" over themselves as complete and absolute (such seemed to be the case with the earlier mentioned Ms. Herald). Often these people think in either-or, right-wrong, good-bad or all-or-nothing terms. They are frequently on the defensive often feeling the need to guard against the usurpation of their power to control their lives. Toward the other end of the continuum, we see persons who experience their "right" over themselves as very important but not absolute. These people are more inclusive in their thought processes relying more frequently on both-and categories. They see that others have a claim on their sovereignty and that their understanding of what is right always needs to be tempered by the will of others. Again, Ms. Shatner seemed to fall toward this end of this continuum.

The Irresponsible/Responsible spoke deals with the amount of ownership one experiences for the decisions that are made. Toward the Irresponsible end of the continuum spoke we often see rather depressive, passive-aggressive persons. For example, when confronted with the option of undergoing painful therapy to fight their disease, if left alone, they usually would decide against therapy. If pushed by others, they may go along with the therapy to avoid the pain of being pushed. However, these people experience very little shared responsibility with physician or family for the uncomfortable process of battling the illness. Instead they almost totally assign this responsibility to others and often experience passive-aggressive anger towards these others when things do not go smoothly (such was the case with our Ms. Johnson). The more one leans toward the Responsible end of the continuum spoke, however, the more resilient and assertive he or she is. These persons are usually quite direct in expressing their feelings. They responsibly own their part in decision-making and in the process of their therapy. They assertively work as a co-partner with their physician and with others involved in their care. When things do not go smoothly, they resiliently look for new ways to encounter their struggle. Ms. Shatner, for example, managed to throw a milkshake party for her friends when she could no longer tolerate solid food as a result of chemotherapy.

The fourth dynamic, the Deterministic/Creative spoke, is perhaps more obviously related to one's sense of spirituality than the other three. It has to do with how one understands the way the universe is made and operates. It suggests to one what is ultimately possible in this life. The more Deterministic one is the more fatalistic (remember Mr. Smith and, again, Ms. Herald). There does not seem to be much freedom in life since happenings by and large are predetermined. This person's God often is seen as either quite distant (usually as a Prime Mover or as a Heavenly Puppeteer) or as an intimate but harsh paternalistic Judge (one who rules by coercion or force and may or may not be quite capricious). Persons who are more toward the Creative end of the continuum spoke function as though there is freedom in life, and they believe their contribution importantly affects the ultimate outcome of the universal web of existence. For example, the growthful influence Ms. Shatner had on her children. God for these persons is quite imminent, graceful, loving and supporting. They very clearly experience themselves to be in a co-creating relationship with the Divine.

CONCLUDING COMMENTS

It would seem that seriously ill persons often move freely on the four-spoked continuum throughout different stages of their illness. One side of the overall continuum (the Open-Relative-Responsible-Creative side) would seem to point more toward "possibility" in life. It invites one into ambiguity while encouraging hope. Such was the case with Ms. Shatner. The other side (the Isolated-Absolute-Irresponsible-Deterministic side) suggests the "limitations" of life, forcing one to constrict or partialize reality. Again, decision-making in the seriously ill largely seems to be a function of one entertaining "possibility" but acting out of "limitation." As circumstances change, seriously ill persons quite often will realign their continuum profile to deal with varying degrees of threat and security. Just before she died, even Ms. Johnson did seem to find some peace in accepting the inevitability of her condition.

Finally, the closing word to this discussion hopefully is a freeing word. While all in the human community are bound to illness and physical demise, let us remember that many options are available in how we approach these events and assign meaning to them. Better understanding of how seriously ill persons make decisions can increase depth, creativity and flexibility both within them as well as in those close to them. Defining various processes in life allows us to enter more fully into life, savoring the struggle to embrace yet new and unintegrated moments of reality. In so doing, I believe we may draw closer to God.

> The tragedy of life is not death, but what dies inside while we are living. . . . We must recognize that we get our basic energy not from turbines but from hope.[4]
>
> *Norman Cousins*

NOTES

1. Sören Kierkegaard, *Life*, as found in *Bartlett's Familiar Quotations: Fifteenth and 125th Anniversary Edition*, John Bartlett, ed. (Boston: Little Brown, 1980).

2. Ernest Becker, *The Denial of Death* (New York: The Free Press, A Division of Macmillan Publishing Co., Inc., 1973), p. 266.

3. Calvin S. Hall, *A Primer of Freudian Psychology* (New York: A Mentor Book published by The New American Library of World Literature, Inc., 1954), p. 28.

4. Quote comes from an informal conversation with a friend who was discussing Cousins' work.

AIDS and Pastoral Care

Charles W. Kessler, MDiv

SUMMARY. Based on a biblical understanding of caring for those whom society fails to nurture, this paper describes a ministry to and with persons with AIDS, focusing on grief work, levels of alienation, and reconciliation in the community. Extensive case description is included as illustration.

INTRODUCTION:
PASTORAL CARE PRESUPPOSITIONS

For fourteen years, my ministry has been devoted to hospital chaplaincy at the New England Deaconess Hospital in Boston, Massachusetts. For the past three years, ministry to persons with AIDS has become a priority for me. Initially, I want to share my personal understanding of chaplaincy, the ministry of pastoral care. For me, the understanding is Biblically-based. Secondly, out of this pastoral care perspective, I want to discuss ministry to persons with AIDS.

Over the course of years, Old and New Testament Biblical imagery has become increasingly important to me as a means of comprehending the meaning and value of pastoral care-giving. The prophetic tradition of the Old Testament provides one of the primary resources for my understanding of pastoral care. In reading the prophetic literature, I am left with the impression that one of the primary sins of society which the prophets condemned was the failure

Charles W. Kessler, New England Deaconess Hospital, 185 Pilgrim Road, Boston, MA 02215.

Portions of this paper were first given at the World Council of Churches Consultation on AIDS, Geneva, Switzerland, June 1986.

of society to nurture. In Chapter 1, verse 16 of the book of Isaiah, the prophet challenges the community: "Cease to do evil, learn to do good, seek justice, correct oppression; defend the fatherless, plead for the widow." And in verse 23 of this same chapter of Isaiah, the sin of the nation is identified: "They do not defend the fatherless, and the widow's cause does not come to them."

Defending the fatherless and pleading for the widow means taking good care of those in society who are most vulnerable, most powerless, and who already bear some of the saddening wounds of life. The society which fails to nurture is the one which does not take care of the vulnerable and the helpless. The society which fails to nurture is the one which perpetuates oppression.

In offering pastoral care, one of my values is to provide a context of nurturing support for people who suffer. I see pastoral care as a ministry which seeks to be a fulfillment of the prophetic call for a compassionate and nurturing social structure, however small and well-defined that social structure may be either in a one-to-one relationship with someone who is ill, or in the relationship with the important others of an ill person.

The second scriptural image which I find quite important is the portrayal of the last judgment scene from the 25th Chapter of Matthew. Beginning in verse 34 are these words:

> Come, O blessed of my Father, inherit the Kingdom prepared for you from the foundation of the world; for I was hungry and you gave me food, I was thirsty and you gave me drink, I was a stranger and you welcomed me, I was naked and you clothed me, I was sick and you visited me, I was in prison and you came to me.

Here in New Testament language are the themes of reaching out in ways which are nurturing to those in need. There is affirmation of caring for those who are powerless and vulnerable. There is affirmation for being with those who are imprisoned, those people who by the standards of society may be considered criminal. Christ is present where there is need, where there is illness, where there is alienation from self, where there is alienation from society.

THE AIDS EXPERIENCE AND MINISTRY
AT NEW ENGLAND DEACONESS HOSPITAL

In the past three years, I have been involved in the pastoral care of more than seventy-five people with AIDS. I have worked with many family members, friends and lovers of AIDS patients. Not all of the AIDS patients have been either homosexual or male. Some of the AIDS patients were women who were infected through intravenous drug use. One woman was infected by a former boyfriend who was a carrier unaware of that fact. Still another young woman in her early 20s was diagnosed after giving birth to her first child. Soon after birth, the child began to exhibit symptoms of AIDS. Shortly after the infant was diagnosed, the mother developed pneumocystis pneumonia and died of this infection. This young mother had been infected by a blood transfusion given during oral surgery four years earlier. In Boston, as in every other community where it is found, AIDS kills men, women and children.

At the time of this writing, the great majority of people I have seen with AIDS have either been homosexual men or intravenous drug users. Pastoral care to members of these groups is complicated by the fact that these people often experience deep alienation from church and society. Historically, the Church has offered condemnation and criticism, rather than support and affirmation. Building a pastoral relationship in this context means transcending alienation.

I want to share the story of one young man whom I met at the end of December 1985. He was 28 years old and I will call him John, though his real name is different. His nurse had asked me to visit him because he seemed rather lonely and isolated. John's home was many hundreds of miles away. Except for some volunteers from the AIDS Action Committee of Boston, he saw no familiar people. I introduced myself to John and simply inquired how he was doing. He was willing to talk to me, and share some of the difficulties he experienced being both ill and financially dependent on strangers. John told me about his family who lived in a small town in northern New England. Though his parents were supportive of him, they were afraid to have him come to his hometown for medical care since they feared that people in their small community would ostracize all of them. Therefore John was in Boston receiving medical treatment, but lonely for those who cared about him deeply.

In this first conversation, John's manner was very serious and intense. After about twenty minutes it appeared that he had shared about as much as he needed, so I told him that I would leave momentarily. When I got up to leave, I went over to John and shook his hand. Suddenly the intensity on his face broke and he smiled. It struck me as ironic that my departure evoked the smile while my presence had stimulated the utmost sobriety.

Two days later I saw John again. He was dressed and waiting for a ride to take him to the house in Boston where he had been staying. John was being discharged. We spoke only for about one minute. There was barely time to wish him well as his ride came.

About a month later, I saw a newly placed medical precautions sign by the door of one of the single rooms in the hospital. This sign often is one of the first indications I have of a person with AIDS. I discovered that John had been readmitted, but this time he was much more ill than before. When I knocked at the door of his room, he looked at me and said, "I was hoping you would come. I am very frightened." When I came close to him, there was a look of panic in his eyes. "John, can you tell me why you're so frightened right now?" "When I was in before, I just had ARC. Now I have AIDS. Since I saw you I've been diagnosed with both Kaposi's and pneumocystis. I knew you could get one. I didn't know you could get both. I'm afraid I'm going to die soon, and I don't know how to pray. Will you pray with me?"

John and I prayed together every day for the several weeks he was in the hospital. Whenever he wanted me to pray with him, I asked him what he wanted me to pray about. He would tell me. The content of each prayer was fundamentally his own, and he would repeat the words after me. We often prayed in thanksgiving for his parents and friends: "O God, I thank you for my mother and my father, and for the understanding, love and care they have given me through the years. O God, I thank you for my friends, and for the wonderful ways in which they support and sustain me. Truly, they are a holy gift in my life." We prayed for his nurses and physicians: "O God, thank you for those who minister to my body, those who seek to help me feel well again." We prayed for deliverance from fear and for God's support on the journey through illness: "O God, do not leave me alone in my fear, but be my steady companion. And though, dear God, the days of my life may be short, may each day that I have be filled with an eternity's worth of love and caring." There was a healing of spirit as John claimed the reality of God's love for him.

When John was finally well enough to leave the hospital, we talked about the first time we had met, that time when his face was guarded and carried no smile. He said that when he first met me and knew that I was a chaplain, he was afraid I was going to preach at him and tell him that he was a horrible person as other clergy had done. When I did not preach at him but simply shook his hand, he began to trust. Alienation had been transcended.

John was homosexual. For this reason he expected condemnation from me and others. Sexuality is one of God's gifts to each of us, regardless of its orientation. The fact is that when sexuality becomes a focus for disapproval in the eyes of the community, whether the community is the Church, the society, or the individual's family, then it is indeed like a prison. People cannot "help" their sexuality. It should not require forgiveness. That seems inappropriate. It simply requires acceptance. The Gospel of Matthew again comes to mind: "I was in prison and you came to me." Society creates its prisons, and our call as Christians is to go to the inner spaces of imprisonment with compassion and care. Sexual orientation should not have to be one of the prisons of this life.

GRIEF WORK: A MAJOR COMPONENT IN HELPING PEOPLE WITH AIDS

A major task of a hospital chaplain is helping people cope with their grief. The very first AIDS patient with whom I worked in depth was a young Puerto Rican man, whom I will call Luiz. He was the father of a three-year-old son.

His nurse had asked me to see him, because one of his close friends had died the previous day in a room directly across the hall from where Luiz was. Luiz was at a point of despair. I felt rather nervous walking into his room which was filled with silent, frightened people. When I introduced myself, Luiz invited me to sit down. He looked me in the eye and said, "Why should I go on? My friend has died and I am dying too. I don't know why I should struggle anymore." I responded to him: "This sickness, it's been a very hard struggle for you." He looked so sad, and simply said, "Yes." Then he added, "My friend suffered so terribly." I asked him gently if he would tell me something about his friend who had been so valuable. He described a sensitive person who had suffered greatly, in a manner which seemed undeserved.

Luiz also began to share some of his own sense of loss about his own life. He worried about his son, and felt the heavy loss of not being able to see him grow to manhood. He grieved a great deal that day, and was able to relinquish some of his sense of despair. He was able to claim the real love and affection of his friends and family. He came to a point of being able to say that in spite of his sufferings, it was really worthwhile trying to stay alive.

In offering pastoral care or any type of support to a person with AIDS, grief issues are always of central importance. Giving up life, career, family, friends, hopes, dreams, at a point in time which should either be the springtime of life, or the early summer of life, is an immense loss. The grieving of people with AIDS deserves the most kind and respectful care.

WORKING THROUGH THE THREE LEVELS OF ALIENATION

No chaplain or care-giver offering support to a person with AIDS can long miss the fact that many feel a profoundly deep sense of alienation. This alienation can be experienced in relation to God, in relation to self, in relation to community. Supporting reconciliation on each of these levels of relationship is the pastoral task.

As a chaplain, I meet people who describe feeling alienated from God. Luiz, who was mentioned above, grew up in Puerto Rico. The religious value system, as well as the culture in his native land was very macho. As a homosexual, the value system had him damned by definition. Over the months I knew him, we talked about God, talked about death, and what God might have in store for each of us. At a much later time I learned that I had said something important to this young man as he sought to come to terms with God. I simply said to him one day, that I thought God was infinitely more understanding and forgiving of each of us than we are of ourselves. With evident enthusiasm, Luiz told each of his friends for days that Chaplain Kessler thought God was more forgiving than people were.

What seemed to happen in a parallel fashion in the life of Luiz, was that as he experienced himself being valued and prized by his network of friends and family, he was able to begin to believe that God could love him, accept him, and prize him too. His spirit found a holy reconciliation.

Again, because I am a chaplain, people sometimes tell me of their alienation from God, yet the real message is that they feel alienated from themselves. A few weeks before Easter 1986, I met a 33-year-old man in the Deaconess Hospital whose first words gave me an indication of deep personal alienation, yet his words were theological. He was on a respirator and very laboriously wrote on a pad of paper that he was not afraid to die. He fervently hoped that someday he might be able to sit at the foot of the throne of God. But he felt that he was not really worthy. He believed that God found him unworthy. I told him that I was not as certain as he that God found him unworthy at all, but that I was fairly certain that he did not find himself to be a worthy person. He then wrote that he had struggled with a life-long sense of not being valuable.

The description of his life which he and others gave me in the days which followed suggested that he lived out of a sincere compassion for others. This young man had my acceptance, and that seemed to help him find a different quality of peacefulness in himself.

He had been newly diagnosed with AIDS, presenting with a pneumocystis infection, and the medications normally used to combat that pneumonia failed. He had only three weeks to come to terms with AIDS, and with his dying. He died the evening before Easter.

Some of this young man's deep sense of unworthiness and alienation from himself was rooted in feelings about his sexual orientation. He had internalized much of the prejudice and homophobia of his society.

Often people with AIDS experience the acute loneliness of being alienated from family and friends. This is heartbreaking to see because the grief of losing support networks is staggering. Sharing the news that one has AIDS with important family members and friends is a process which can be difficult and traumatic. The risk and fear of abandonment is particularly intense. Sometimes it means being candid about sexual orientation to people who do not know, to people who may not be pleased, to people who may reject. Supporting a person with AIDS during a period when trying to overcome secretiveness and the perceived alienation from community is very important.

In March of this year, I was asked to see a young man from central Massachusetts. The nurse who asked me to see him told me that he was newly diagnosed and was "very emotional and needed to talk to someone." I was told that none of his family or friends knew of his diagnosis. When I met this young man, who was 27, he told me that he was frightened. As we talked, it was apparent that the fear centered on sharing a frightening diagnosis. He was not afraid to share life-style. That was already known. We began to sort through ways of telling people. He felt confident that some very close friends would support him. He was less certain about his family. We talked through a strategy of building initially a community of support for himself with those friends he most trusted. When he felt secure with his friends, it would then be the right time to approach his family. The strategy worked. The close friends were reliable and supportive, and gave him necessary strength to talk to his parents. After this young man's father had visited him in the hospital he told me, "My father doesn't talk to me very much. He never has. But I know from the way he looks at me, whether he cares or not. My dad cares about me. He's with me in this."

This young man left our hospital hoping to have several months of relatively good health. He returned in less than two weeks with severe intestinal disease and progressive wasting. Very quickly he began facing another form of alienation, the alienation of dying. With the disintegration of his body he felt the disintegration of his life. He overcame a fear of his own grieving, as he shared the depth of his sorrow. For his young age, he was quite mature. Regarding medical treatment, he did not want to be maintained needlessly if there could be no real quality in his living. For him quality living meant independence. He had such dignity. This young man represents in part some of the incredibly extravagant waste of good life which this disease of AIDS creates.

RECONCILIATION IN THE COMMUNITY

Just as seeking reconciliation is a primary task in the one-to-one pastoral care of persons with AIDS, a major task for the Church in the face of this disease is to work for reconciliation in the entire community. AIDS is a catalyst bringing to the fore some of the worst fears and prejudices associated with the groups most affected by the disease. Addressing the fears and prejudices of society at large becomes an important part of the ministry of reconciliation. On one level there are the fears of the disease. Educating people with accurate information about AIDS, its modes of transmission, as well as detailed and frank information indicating how people become at risk is imperative.

Moving beyond the facts of the disease, we have to work with those attitudes in society which are hostile and prejudiced. Contrary to views expressed by the spokespersons of some of the more conservative segments of the Christian community, reconciliation does not mean that a person with AIDS, usually a homosexual person, must renounce life choices and life values, including the love of significant others. Such an act would not be reconciliation, but capitulation to an aggressive moralizing. I am aware of a situation in our hospital a few years ago, when a priest visiting from an outside parish told a man dying of AIDS that he could not expect any mercy from God unless he renounced his lover. This response devastated both the young man who was dying, as well as his lover. Another priest, who later established a genuinely supportive relationship with these two men, described the first priest as being the real sinner by virtue of his insensitivity.

We have to work toward a greater acceptance of people by people, a greater acceptance of the diversity of human sexuality. In the course of this disease, I have seen a number of homosexual couples facing the illness with the faithfulness, tenderness, and bravery associated often in the common mind with the personal fidelity of a devoted husband or wife. We need to help the Church and society in general be reconciled to the fact that God has created a great diversity of sexuality and sexual response. Our job is not to condemn people for the direction of their sexuality. Our task is to help people make choices in relationship, as to the use of their sexuality, so that it in fact can be the life affirming, intimacy building holy gift it was intended to be. Even if we look at Genesis, Eve was created because Adam was lonely. Reproduction was not the issue. Companionship and intimacy were key. Reconciliation means change, growth, greater understanding and appreciation on everyone's part, so that people can in truth love one another.

In Boston, we have embarked on an effort to raise the level of awareness of people in our churches through the work of an Ecumenical Task Force on AIDS. Among other things, the Task Force has sponsored a number of monthly healing services which have been held in various parishes throughout the Metropolitan area. Often a parish hosting such a service will go through a process of education about AIDS, and about the pastoral needs of people with AIDS. It is slow work at a grass roots level, but we are seeing some deepening of compassion in the religious community of our city.

A LOOK TO THE FUTURE

The long term projections about AIDS are most sobering. By 1991, it is estimated that 145,000 people in the U.S. alone will be sick with AIDS.* It is estimated by the Public Health Service that the cost of treating these people will be somewhere between $8 and $16 billion for that year alone. We all know that the AIDS epidemic will get much worse.

The challenge to the Church is obvious. AIDS demands our attention. The sufferers from this disease need our love, support and prayer. Those who are frightened need education and understanding. Efforts to find a vaccine and/or a cure deserve our support. To be indifferent to AIDS is to invite a public health calamity unprecedented in modern times.

---

* By 1991, the cumulative total since 1981 of persons with AIDS in the United States is projected at 270,000. Of that number, it is estimated that in 1991, 145,000 will be alive and suffering, and 125,000, will already have died.

Stroke:
Its Mechanics and Dynamics in Ministry to Patients

Cecilia Baranowski, RSM

SUMMARY. Strokes are one of America's major health problems. While there is progress toward prevention, the health care chaplain must understand the basic mechanics of stroke as a context for theological reflection and ministry. This article outlines the physical dynamics and effects of stroke as well as the stories of ministry to three stroke patients.

Stroke . . . say this word slowly and be aware of the sound it makes; be aware of any feelings that may surface in you. In the course of my ministry I have found that stroke is a word that strikes terror in the heart of a family who has just heard the physician tell them their loved one has suffered a stroke. Immediate thoughts center on mortality, on paralysis, on how much recovery to expect. And the grieving process, described by Elisabeth Kübler-Ross, begins not only for the family but also for the patient who rebels against his/her losses.

Strokes are one of our major health problems. They afflict hundreds of thousands of people every year. Yet today the outlook for stroke patients is more hopeful than ever before. Because of advances in treatment and rehabilitation, many patients are being restored to a useful life.

Progress has been made toward prevention. Often doctors can detect warning signs and symptoms and take measures to reduce the

Sr. Cecilia Baranowski, Chaplain, Pastoral Care Department, St. Anne's Hospital Corporation, 795 Middle St., Fall River, MA 02721-1798.

59

risk of a serious stroke. In some people preventive surgery can be performed.

This paper has a dual purpose. The first is to present the story of three stroke patients and the theological implications of their losses. The second is to define the mechanics of stroke and its effects.

MINISTRY TO PATIENTS

I would like to introduce you to three people—Bill, Elsie, and Tom—who have suffered a stroke. These people are left hemiplegics, the most recent patients with whom I have had extended contact. Their names have been changed to protect their privacy. This is not only their story but also my story as I ministered and continue to minister to them. All quotes are from verbatim accounts of my visits.

Patients with a right CVA are predominant in Leader North where I work. In conversation with members of the rehab team I was informed that this was the most common type of stroke. I would have liked to include the story of a right hemiplegic but lacking such a patient to work with I was unable to do so.

Ministry to Bill

Bill is a 56-year-old married man who suffered a mild myocardial infarction on September 11, 1985. He was admitted to The Williamsport Hospital. Following his cardiac catheterization he stroked on September 27. I met him November 13 when he was admitted to the nursing home for a proposed stay of two months of rehab before returning to his home. His actual stay was two weeks for reasons which will become evident as his story unfolds.

I was particularly interested in Bill because he was, at that time, the youngest stroke patient whom I had seen. He made me aware of my own vulnerability. As we initially talked he said, "It was terrible. I just couldn't believe it. My arm and leg were gone. There was nothing there."

For me I could only imagine the horror of waking up one day and feeling half of my body had disappeared. The fear, the frustration, intermingled with the denial of what is, can only lead to a deep seated anger. It takes time for the patient to accept the fact that he is not okay; that there is something wrong; that he can improve with effort. The length of the depression immediately following a stroke is individualized and Bill resisted therapy for about three weeks while in the rehab program at The Williamsport Hospital. He told me, "It took a long time to realize I had to cooperate with the therapists. They couldn't get me walking until I realized it depended on me."

Realizing he could regain some of his independence, he became determined and made sufficient progress within the next month to be discharged to a nursing home for further rehab. His wife was determined to take him home and care for him when he was ready to go.

Bill has organic flattened affect. It was difficult to determine what emotion he was feeling as he spoke. As for his wife, she fluctuated between depression and lack of realism in the two weeks I had seen her, bursting into tears each time we spoke, torn between her desire to take him home and the realization that he was going to be more difficult to care for than she had initially realized.

Both husband and wife were in denial, desperately wanting to believe the situation would be greatly improved when Bill returned home. During one visit Bill told me, "A little movement came back to my leg. If I can just lock the brace (long leg) I will walk." And his wife confided, "I'll be able to get him in and out of the car okay. Then we can get out."

He was a smoker and several times had cigarette burns on his left arm. (He had left neglect.) When questioned he would reply, "I scratched myself. That's okay." His wife, too, would concur with what he said even though she sat with him in the smoking room each day. Perhaps this came from the fear that he would not be discharged if the truth were known.

At times I became frustrated with the denial of both patient and wife. Everything was not okay and things would not return to normal when Bill went home. Bill will never be the man he was nor would she find it easy to live with his impulsiveness and lack of insight into his disability. On the other hand I felt sorry for Bill knowing that at home he would still be facing anger, frustration, and loneliness. It would be difficult for his wife, too, but together they had to discover this.

One week after his admission, Bill was overcome by feelings of isolation and loneliness. "It's not fair for me to be here with all these old people. I don't have any company. My friends won't even come and visit me here. They did at the hospital — every night." As we talked about the loneliness his real fears began to surface. "These old people are pathetic. No one wants to see them."

So I tried to get him to project into the future. He became fearful of losing his control; of losing his independence; of becoming more debilitated. I asked him what he thought of when he saw all these older people around him and he sat in thoughtful silence. Then I ventured to ask him how he saw himself in 30 years. In a monotone voice he replied, "I'm never going to be like that. I'll never give up my house. I'm not going to get old like they are." And he sat and cried and my heart ached for him.

Concerning his feelings about being in the nursing home he said, "I have nothing to look forward to. I have nothing to do — therapy in the morning and then again in the afternoon. After that it's just sitting." His desperation being evident and concern for his mental health prompted the staff to draw up discharge plans and Bill went home.

Bill is a man who needs to be in control. He was a church goer until he had a difference of opinion with the pastor several years ago. Not being able to have his own way, he stopped going to church.

Organized religion was, for him, a chance to get together with his friends. He still looked to his friends for company, for support, for recreation, for affirmation. "I liked to go to church. I would meet my friends there."

I suspect Bill has unresolved feelings about God. He has lost his independence, his sense of control, his sense of who he is. He can't have his way. He is severely limited.

As for myself, it upset me to see such a young man so incapacitated; a young man who refused to accept the reality of his situation and was consequently unable to compensate for his losses; a young man who believed that going home would solve all his problems.

Biblically I think of Jesus being tempted in the wilderness (Matt.

4:1-10). After every great moment in life there comes a reaction. It is in the reaction we must be careful for it can make us or break us. Jesus spent 40 days in the wilderness. The devil tempted Him in His weakened condition. And in the weakened condition He was able to withstand the tempter. Jesus's struggle with the devil was an interior one. The tempter comes through our thoughts and desires.

Bill struggles with the temptation that life as he now experiences it does not have to be, that it will get better when certain conditions will be satisfied. I see him adding more conditions as he continues to meet more frustrations. Unlike Jesus he cannot say to the tempter, "Be gone. I am who I am and will use what I have."

Ministry to Elsie

Elsie is an 87-year-old widow who was married for 58 years and is childless. In October of 1984, while residing in Atlantic City, she suffered her first stroke and was placed in a nursing home. When she became ambulatory she returned to Williamsport to live with her sister. Upon the death of her sister she moved in with a sister-in-law. On December 2, 1985, she stroked again.

I first met Elsie when she came to the nursing home on December 20. The left side of her mouth drooped, she had a blank look on her face; she did not converse but answered questions with a yes or no only with much encouragement. She was paralyzed, lethargic, confused, forgetful, and aphasic.

Two months after her admission she still remains paralyzed, lethargic, forgetful, confused, and aphasic. Her affect is flat and her face is expressionless. She is unaware of her deficits, has not regained any feeling on her left side, has gross left sided neglect, has a very short attention span, and is unmotivated.

Due to her deficits my ministry to her takes a different form. When visiting Elsie I sit on her right side, facing her. Even then I must sometimes shift my position slightly to get her attention. Touch is very important. It reassures the patient and establishes contact. In Elsie's case it is my best means of communicating with her. When I have her attention I hold her hand and talk to her. Initially there was no response. Recently she has begun to squeeze my hand.

My verbal communication with her is simple. I ask questions to which she can respond with a yes or no or one word. Knowing some of her history from her chart I talk about her past. Her long-term memory has not returned. She appears to be forgetful.

She consistently tells me she is fine, has no problems, is doing well in therapy, and walks fine. When asked to let me hold her left hand she gives me the right. If I visit when she has returned from therapy she is much too tired. Her eyelids are closing; she yawns; her head droops. Yet she tells me she hasn't done anything in therapy that tired her.

I take the time to sit with her and let her know she is not alone; that I care about her. I can only presume that she may be frightened, anxious, frustrated, lonely, discouraged. By my attentiveness I hope to bring her some comfort.

At this point in time I can not help her to struggle to find meaning for her life; to struggle with the question of why this has happened; to clarify her relationship to God. Through my ministry I try to bring her a sense of the love, the gentleness, the care, the concern, the comfort of a loving God.

Elsie reminds me of Peter denying Christ. "And the servant girl, seeing him in the light of the fire said, 'This man was with Him.' He denied it saying, 'Woman, I do not know Him'" (Luke 22:56-57).

This was not the real Peter who cracked beneath the tension; the real Peter who protested his loyalty in the upper room; the real Peter who drew his sword to protest. Neither is Elsie the real woman who consistently says she is fine; that nothing is wrong; that her therapy is going well.

I may never know the real Elsie. She may never again know herself as she was or is. The Elsie that is today is the Elsie that I bless and uplift to my God.

Ministry to Tom

Tom is 71 and married. He and his wife have no children. Tom had a career as a draftsman specializing in engine design. He served in the navy during the first World War. After being discharged he

devoted time to caring for his mother who was widowed and af-
flicted with cancer. He married when he was 39.

In the spring of 1984 Tom had a myocardial infarct. He was sent
to Robert Packer Hospital where he had undergone a double bypass
and had a defective valve replaced. In September of 1984 he had a
CVA and spent two months in the rehab program at The Williamsport Hospital. This is where I initially met Tom.

His progress was very slow and laborious due to his medical
condition and his attitude. He had a reputation for being angry,
rude, demanding, hostile, uncooperative, and self-pitying. His wife
was at wit's end knowing she could not cater to him nor take him
home. Nursing home placement was inevitable.

In November of 1984 he was admitted to the nursing home. It
was here that I became better acquainted with Tom. From the fall to
the summer was a very difficult period for both of us. Tom continued to be angry, rude, demanding, uncooperative, and self-centered. Because of his behavior my feelings would swing from frustration to sympathy to anger. The more I tried to be patient and
understanding the more demanding he became.

When I would leave his room after a visit he would literally shout
with full gusto, "Sister, help me. Sister, help me. Sister, where are
you?" and continue until I would return. He was full of self-pity,
crying that he would never walk again; that no one understood what
he was going through. He resisted any and all suggestions of what
he might do to relieve his boredom.

Finally by early summer he started to show some progress. Although he could not walk and probably never would be able to, he
was beginning to show progress in aiding in his transfer from bed to
wheelchair and vice versa.

He was determined to go home and his wife agreed to take him,
alone, without benefit of support services. In early July he was
discharged to home. Ten days later his wife brought him back. She
was unable to care for him physically and, I suspect, emotionally.

This put Tom into a depression. For several weeks he sat in his
room, in his wheelchair, staring out the window crying and being
very irritable. Strangely enough he would not and still does not
admit to anger at his wife. Whenever he mentions her it is always in
the context of "I love her very much. She is a strong-willed

woman. She just couldn't handle me. I was too much for her." But more about this later.

I believe he is dealing with the fear of losing her. She is a daily visitor coming twice a day to help him with meals. Without her he would have nothing. She does provide for his material needs. But she *is* a strong-willed woman. She does not give in to his whims and demands nor does she allow him to manipulate her. I am sure she has had to learn how to brace herself and not allow herself to get worn down playing his game.

Observing the two of them together she appears to be very business like, somewhat aloof and sarcastic. He says to her, "I'm much better now. I'd be able to get out of bed if I had a bar like I do here." To which she replies, "You told me that before I took you home. Then you wouldn't give me any help at all. No way; you stay here."

As a child Tom did not have a stable religious foundation. He started off as a Methodist, went to the Christian Scientist Church with his aunt, and then settled down in the Lutheran Church. When describing his childhood and teen years he said, "I dabbled around in religion. Just couldn't find something to satisfy me."

That dissatisfaction continues up to the present and comes out as blaming others, self-pity, lack of motivation, and anger. Tom blames the medical profession for his condition. In his own words, "I had the heart surgery because I changed doctors. I was going to Dr. A. He took care of me. I liked him. But then he sent me to Dr. B. for my heart. He did a catheterization on me. Then he said I needed surgery. If I said no I wouldn't be like this today. I would be okay. In Robert Packer they did a job on me with blood thinners. After I was taking them I fell down. That's what caused the stroke." The blame also reaches out to those who have died and left him to his own resources. "My aunt was a Christian Scientist. I'd be well if she were alive." And then, "If my mother had been alive this never would have happened. She was a good nurse. She would have told me whether I needed the surgery or not."

Besides the tears he sheds on a daily basis because he is at the nursing home, tears flow freely over a variety of topics which highlight his self-pitying stance. His brother-in-law, an Alzheimer's patient, is also in the same nursing home. "Look at Will. He's better off than I am. His mind is gone. He doesn't know what's going on. My mind is okay. I can't take it."

And again he mentions his mother, "My father died when I was in high school. Then I joined the navy. When I got out of the service I stayed home and took care of my mother. She had cancer. I stayed with her until she died. Now look at me."

One day he was crying as I found him sitting in his room. "Look how nice it is outside and I'm stuck in here."

Christmas was a particularly painful time for him. "I couldn't go home. My wife can't handle me. And no one was around. The rest of the family was out of town. So my wife spent the day here with me but it's not the same as being home."

Tom's lack of motivation is seen in the many excuses he makes. Initially when he complained of boredom I talked to him trying to discover his interests and could find nothing that was now of interest to him. He discounted everything as being impractical, impossible, too much trouble.

After his readmission in July the excuses continued. So, too, did his self-pitying attitude. He has said so many times, "I can't move anyplace by myself." When I encourage him to practice maneuvering his wheelchair to gain a measure of independence he replies, "But this leg rest is in the way." If I offer to have someone take it off for him or to do it myself he says, "Oh, I don't want to bother anyone. They're all busy."

Tom is an animal lover. He sat by his window during the fall hoping to see some deer on the hillside. He also likes to watch the birds. "I want to be outside and watch the birds," he says often. When encouraged to practice getting around in his chair so he can get outside himself when the weather gets warmer, he says, "But that's such a long time off." Then he tells me how much he enjoyed feeding the birds and watching them eat. To which I suggested he put a bird feeder on his window—one that has a suction cup. "I wouldn't be able to see the birds anyway. My roommate sits by the window in the morning. I'd have to get a different room."

He was an avid golf player. "Even when I got back from Packer I still played golf. But now I can't." Suggestions about keeping up with golf news, watching tournaments on television, are all met with resistance. "That's not the same."

His anger goes in two directions—at his wife and God. He has mentioned several times that "Mary can't handle me. Mary is a strong-willed woman." He didn't go home for Christmas because his wife couldn't handle him. He cried about this several days before and after Christmas. "Mary paints and wallpapers. She's a real workhorse; real strong." Each time he talks about her physical strength he always ends the same, "She can't handle me. I'm too heavy for her."

On one occasion his sister had visited him. When I went to him shortly afterwards he was crying, "My sister says if Mary takes me home she would help with my care. But Mary won't. She's too independent." The theme of his wife's independence is a frequent one.

There is also anger at God. "Why is God punishing me? I was a good man. I never even shot a squirrel." Talking to him about a loving God elicited responses such as, "Yah, if God really loved His son He wouldn't have let him die. That was a mean thing to do." He was sure that wicked people were blessed. "Look at Hitler. Look at all the people he killed and he wasn't sick a day in his life. And he's not the only one. There are others who had it good, too. I don't know what I did to deserve this punishment."

There is also anger at the role reversal he has experienced. "Mary paints and wallpapers. Now she shovels the snow. She does things I can't do anymore. She is so good."

Denial of his condition is also seen as unrealistic expectations. "I am going to walk. I can't stay in this chair the rest of my life. When my brace gets fixed I will be able to walk. I'm not going to stay here the rest of my life. I am going to go home."

Depression brings with it feelings of helplessness and hopelessness. "I want to go home so much. Doesn't seem that anything is getting better. I'm off therapy now. I'll never get any better." And talk of dying comes with remarks like, "I just want to go home before I die. If I don't walk I'd rather die. I don't want to die but what's left?"

Tom's impulsiveness was highlighted the day the seven astronauts died in the tragic explosion of the Challenger spacecraft. Being a designer of engines I thought he might have some insights that I might stimulate. So I sat and talked with him asking what he thought about the tragedy. He replied, "That was terrible. Their bodies probably fell in the swamps and the alligators got them." I continued expressing thoughts that no one could have survived the explosion. "Oh, yes, they could. Those shuttles are built to withstand a lot." My last remarks expressed the doubt that the cause of the explosion would ever be discovered. But he remained undaunted. "They know what did it. It's liquid oxygen. Anything can set it off, even heat." I left his room feeling depressed.

You may be wondering how ministry to Tom affects me. Believe me, it's not easy. I feel sorry for him. I feel frustrated and disgusted at times. I feel anger and annoyance when he disregards the limits I set for him. I end the visit, say goodbye, stand up to leave and he begins to cry or switches into another topic. His lack of motivation is particularly frustrating.

My saving grace is knowing that a stroke damages the brain, magnifies personality traits, or alters personality; that a stroke patient does not choose a particular behavior.

Tom reminds me of the man at the pool of Bethesda. "'Do you want to be healed?' 'Sir,' the sick man answered, 'I do not have anyone to plunge me into the pool once the water has been stirred up'" (John 5:6-7). Jesus's question may not have been as foolish as it may sound. The man had waited for 38 years. It might well be that his hope had died and he was left with a passive and dull despair. And so Tom waits as did this man. If Tom can find meaning for his life and discover a merciful God in the midst of that life he will be ready, like this man in the gospel story, to get up. Rather than continue to be defeated, his desire and determination can be intensified so that with Christ he can conquer that which now has conquered him.

Now that you have seen the real life struggle of three patients and my role in helping them to adjust and find meaning for their lives I would like to present to you some factual information about the mechanics of stroke, the psychosocial dynamics of the stroke patient and their effects on family and friends, and the role of pastoral care.

STROKE DEFINED

What is a stroke? A stroke or cerebro-vascular accident, also known as a CVA, is not a disease. It occurs when the blood supply to a part of the brain tissue is cut off. As a result the nerve cells in the affected area cease to function. The cerebral nerve cells control the manner in which we receive and interpret sensations. They also control most of our movements. When some of these cells are no longer able to function due to the cessation of the blood supply, the part of the body controlled by these cells also ceases to function. The result may be difficulty in speaking, in seeing, a loss of memory, or the inability to walk. The effects of stroke may be very slight or they may be severe. They may be temporary or they may be permanent. What happens depends in part on which brain cells have been damaged; how widespread the damage is; and how effectively the body can repair its system of supplying blood to the brain; or how rapidly other areas of brain tissue can take over the work of the damaged brain cells.[1]

The person's pre-morbid functioning will determine to some degree how he will react after a stroke. Stroke can mask or magnify personality traits. One patient may struggle to recover while another may resign himself to helplessness. The road to recovery is long and tenuous.

CAUSES OF STROKE

One of the most common causes of stroke is the blocking of a cerebral artery by a clot or thrombus. Sometimes a wandering clot, known as an embolus, is carried in the bloodstream and becomes wedged in a cerebral artery. When a clot plugs a cerebral artery the blood supply is shut off and a stroke occurs.

Little strokes, called trans-ischemic accidents or TIA's, occur when a very small area of the brain tissue is affected. A little stroke can also occur when a large artery is narrowed by atherosclerosis. Atherosclerosis is an abnormal condition of the arteries in which a thick, rough deposit forms on the inner wall of the arteries and gradually narrows the passageway so that the blood flow is slowed.[2] The immediate impact is so slight, a brief dizzy spell or confusion, that people may not be aware of them.

The long term effects are scarcely noticeable at first. Clumsiness in using the hand may show up as a change in handwriting. The patient may become irritable or there may be a personality change. Signs which suggest a TIA should be brought to the physician's attention so that he may decide whether preventive therapy is indicated.

REPAIR SYSTEM

When the blood supply is cut off from an area, the body attempts to repair itself by causing small arteries to expand and take over part of the work of the damaged artery. In this way nerve cells that have been temporarily put out of order may recover. If and when damaged cells recover, that part of the body that has been affected may eventually return to normal. The outlook for recovery is usually better if a stroke has been caused by a clot in a small artery rather than when an artery has ruptured. Regular medical checkups are the best protection against stroke.

PREDISPOSING FACTORS

There are certain predisposing factors which can precipitate a stroke:

1. atherosclerosis—can be controlled by exercise and diet
2. hypertension—uncontrolled high blood pressure increases the risk of cerebral hemorrhage
3. heart disease—good management of heart disease reduces the risk of stroke
4. diabetes—incidence of stroke is increased in diabetics
5. elevated hematocrit (relative increase in the number of red blood cells)—can be treated
6. oral contraceptives
7. family history—hypertension, stroke, or heart disease in the family increases the risk
8. smoking
9. stress—controlled by sensible exercise and regular recreation
10. obesity—relationship between body weight and risk of stroke is suspected but not proven.[3]

WARNING SIGNS

Often physicians can detect signs and symptoms which indicate a stroke is about to occur. Your own body may give warning signs of an impending stroke:

— sudden temporary weakness or numbness of face, arm, or leg
— temporary difficulty or loss of speech
— sudden temporary loss of vision especially in one eye
— episode of double vision
— unexplained headaches or change in pattern of headaches
— temporary dizziness
— recent change in personality or mental ability

If the physician finds these symptoms are caused by blockage of an artery leading to the brain, surgery may be performed to remove the block and ward off a stroke. The removal of blood clots and aneurysms has also been successful in treating strokes.

Drugs that delay clotting of blood or prevent clotting may be prescribed to avert a first stroke or to prevent a second one. A person who has had one stroke is at high risk for another so treatment to reduce risk is important.

RIGHT-SIDED PARALYSIS

The most visible sign of stroke is paralysis on one side of the body. If there is paralysis of the right side, also known as right hemiplegia, there is an injury to the left side of the brain (Figure 1).

A patient with right-sided paralysis is likely to have problems with speech and language. This is called aphasia. Aphasic patients will sometimes be able to understand more than they are able to speak or write.

Society places great emphasis on speech and communication. When a person can't speak or write or be understood there is a tendency to regard him as more disabled than he really is.

Speech and language are different. Language is composed of noises, movements, gestures, and expressions we use to communicate with one another. Speech refers only to a small portion of language, the noises we make with our mouths.[4]

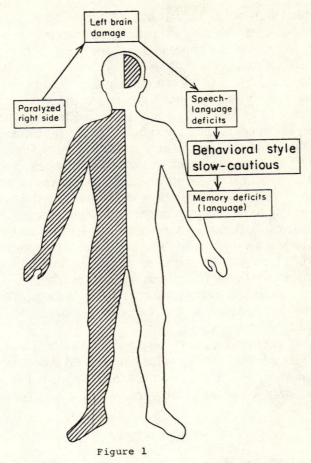

Figure 1

Because a person is unable to speak and be understood, or listen and understand, does not mean he is unable to communicate or understand language. A great deal of communication can be carried on without the use of words. Therefore, the aphasic patient should not be isolated. Demonstration or pantomime are effective methods of communication.

At times the aphasic patient will use unusual words or sounds. If further return of language is not anticipated these words or sounds should be used. Insisting the patient learn the correct word can generate frustration and anger and perhaps cause him to abandon further efforts to communicate.

Many aphasic patients can quickly develop an effective communication by using gestures, groans, swear words, or nonsense sounds. If this language is not responded to the patient may stop trying to communicate. If you insist the patient use a language system that confuses him, he may refuse to communicate at all.

One of the most common errors made when dealing with an aphasic patient is to overestimate his understanding of speech.[5] So much of our communication is nonverbal that the patient may be responding to objects in your hand, your expression, the setting, or the time of day but not your words. The level of understanding can be checked by saying one thing and gesturing another.

When the aphasic's ability to use and understand speech is overestimated, it is easy for frustration, disappointment, and confusion to develop. If you overestimate the patient's speech skills, you may see him as cross, uncooperative, senile, or irrational when you believe he understands you.[6]

Another error is made by giving the patient messages that are too complicated. He might be able to understand short simple messages but miss long or complicated ones. Shouting is not necessary nor is it necessary to use a special voice. When talking keep it simple.

BEHAVIORAL STYLE

In addition to language problems, right hemiplegics have a tendency to be slow, cautious, and disorganized when approaching an unfamiliar problem.[7] This anxious, hesitant style comes as a surprise to family and friends.

The right hemiplegic is likely to need frequent feedback that he is performing correctly. This may become awkward for the caregiver but not for the patient. Too much feedback is better than too little. It must be accurate and frequent, and be given immediately to insure that the patient is learning and performing correctly. Because this type of patient is anxious and cautious he will need many indications of success.

LEFT-SIDED PARALYSIS

Left-sided paralysis indicates damage to the right hemisphere of the brain (Figure 2). The stroke patient with right brain damage will often show difficulty with spatial-perceptual tasks. This refers to the ability to judge size, distance, position, rate of movement, form and the relation of parts to wholes.[8]

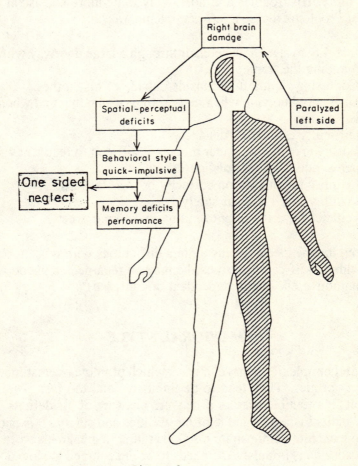

Figure 2

Spatial-perceptual deficits are often overlooked but are as important as speech. Almost all of us have experienced minor spatial-perceptual failure when tired or when concentrating on one task while performing another. Example: expecting another step at the end of a flight of stairs and tripping when it wasn't there; missing the edge of the table with your coffee cup while reading the paper. These are spatial-perceptual errors.

The left hemiplegic is likely to have all of these difficulties plus many more. His troubles are most likely to be more consistent and severe. Problems facing a left hemiplegic are:

1. Inability to steer a wheelchair through a large doorway without bumping the frame.
2. Confusing right/left and inside/outside of his clothes.
3. Difficulty knowing when he is sitting or standing and when he is leaning.
4. Difficulty estimating distances.
5. Losing his place on paper making it difficult to read a newspaper or add a column of figures.
6. Inability to get shirt on correctly or miss buttons.
7. Inability to drive a car safely.
8. Females have inability to put on make up correctly.

When he unexpectedly encounters difficulties with what appears to be simple self-care activities, he may be regarded as uncooperative, unmotivated, overly dependant or confused.[9]

BEHAVIORAL STYLE

"Left hemiplegics behave in ways which promote overestimation of their abilities. They tend to be impulsive and too fast. The left hemiplegic often behaves as if he were unaware of his deficits."[10]

The patient is a poor judge of his abilities and safety. It is necessary to have him demonstrate his skills rather than take his word for it. Because he is impulsive he needs to be encouraged to slow down and to check each step of his task as he completes it. For this reason a great deal of feedback is needed. This feedback needs to be positive. Nagging will discourage him and his performance level will drop.

Left hemiplegics have difficulty understanding visual clues in the environment. For this reason it is necessary to keep the room well-lighted and the environment very simple. A room that is poorly lit or cluttered with a brightly patterned wallpaper may very well be a distraction and hinder performance. Rapid movements of others may also confuse the patient.

ONE-SIDED NEGLECT

Many stroke patients have cuts in their visual field. Right hemiplegics tend to have right field cuts and left hemiplegics tend to have left field cuts. To illustrate – if the left half of each lens is taped you would have difficulty seeing objects left of center. You would learn to turn your head and compensate. Most, but not all stroke patients learn to compensate by turning their heads. Some can't make the adjustment and thereby don't see all parts of an object. This is called neglect and is more problematic for left hemiplegics than for right hemiplegics.

Sometimes the neglect involves signals from all senses on one side. For example, a patient may not recognize his own arm and leg as parts of his body. He may look at the involved arm and leg while he is in bed and become angry because someone is in bed with him.[11]

A patient with serious neglect problems behaves as if he were selectively ignoring all that happens on the impaired side. At times he will divide things he sees at the midline. He may eat everything on one side of the plate and leave the rest. He may read only parts of words.

One-sided neglect may isolate a patient if his unimpaired side is away from the activities going on around him. His unimpaired side should be placed so he can respond to activities around him. Such a patient can become confused when travelling. Being wheeled down and back an unfamiliar hallway he sees only one side going and one side coming. It is as if he has traveled two separate hallways.

Feedback is important. He should be given as much information as possible about his neglected limbs and environment. If neglect is disabling it may be well to modify the environment to compensate for his deficits. Furniture may need to be shifted so that items are on his non-neglected side.

MEMORY

Almost any injury to the brain produces memory problems. The right hemiplegic tends to have memory difficulties associated with language while the left hemiplegic will have problems with spatial-perceptual information. It is also possible to have neither language nor spatial-perceptual deficits and still have significant memory loss. Memory has many components one of which is retention span.

Retention Span

Retention span refers to how much information can be retained by the patient and acted upon or used. A stroke patient has a short retention span. When working with memory deficits the patient's ability to perform can be increased if you:

1. Establish a fixed routine.
2. Keep messages short.
3. Present new information one step at a time.
4. Allow patient to finish one step before proceeding to the next.
5. Give frequent indications of effective progress.
6. Train in settings that resemble the setting in which the behavior is to be practiced.
7. Use memory aides such as appointment books, notes, schedule cards.
8. Use familiar objects and old associations when teaching new tasks.[12]

EMOTIONAL LABILITY

A patient with a recent stroke will show partial loss of his emotional control. He may switch from laughing to crying for no apparent reason. Crying seems to be the most frequent problem. Often excessive crying by the stroke patient is due to the brain damage he has experienced and is not directly connected with his perceived losses.[13]

It is usually possible to tell the difference between loss of emotional control due to brain damage and sadness due to depression. Organic emotional lability has no obvious relationship between the tears and the environment. The emotional behavior is easily interrupted by diverting the patient's attention. Unexpected laughter, flares of anger, or moaning can be interrupted. In the stroke patient feelings and the overt expression of emotion are not always linked as cause and effect.[14]

APHASIA

Aphasia is a technical name given for interference with the comprehension and use of language — a condition which can follow injury to the brain.[15] An aphasic person has a series of problems. The difficulty with language takes a number of forms since language has many forms. Most aphasic patients have some difficulty producing speech. This problem may be so severe that the patient is literally speechless. Or he may have trouble with certain words or phrases.

Sometimes the disorder affects only the understanding of speech but frequently both understanding and production are affected. There may be difficulty in reading, writing, or using numbers. Most patients have difficulty with all of these problems in varying degrees.

The aphasic patient has not lost his language but has lost the ability to recall and use it. So recovery means recalling what has already been learned. Aphasia affects retention and recall. During early stages of the illness there may be no recall at all. This condition usually improves with time. Long term memory returns first. Short term memory takes longer.

The home environment can be an ideal place for helping the aphasic patient recover. It supplies much that is lacking in a hospital — warmth, understanding, familiar surroundings, a helpful family. In general, the best way the family can help its aphasic member is to offer stimulating and understanding companionship.[16]

ATTITUDINAL AND BEHAVIORAL PROBLEMS

Left alone, the patient's progress in language falters and may stop. He is apt to become more withdrawn, anxious, and depressed. It is the individual's motivation and drive that aids in recovery. Stimulation of an understanding family is the means to motivate the patient. Family reactions differ. There may be deep disturbance, over-anxiety, even resentment. These feelings must be examined and evaluated honestly. It is best to hide deep emotions from the patient lest he become depressed. A person who is not emotionally involved can be more effective in aiding recovery. Patients may resent assistance from a spouse due to a fear of losing respect.

It is important to spend time with the patient when his energy and motivation are high. His peaks of interest should be followed. Leaving him alone for certain times permits him to develop a sense of freedom.

As long as those around him remain calm so will he. He should be included in the group even if he doesn't attempt to be sociable. His interest should be aroused. His life history is a good starting place. By trial and error activities that stimulate him will be found. There will be tears and anger when he sees objects that remind him of what he can no longer do.

It is best to accept the patient as he is, ignoring much of his explosiveness and irritability. As he learns to adapt his self-control should increase. As self-centeredness decreases progress is made.

Attention should be paid to specific problems which bother him. This will decrease his anxiety. Success in little things should be praised. Encouragement should be realistic. Everything is not fine and his life will never be the same.

Doing things on his own helps him regain some of his independence. Some patients need a great deal of assistance but this does not mean constant service, catering to whims, or over-solicitude. Steadily decreasing the amount of help offered encourages him to do more for himself. Because of the contacts he makes, his use of language can improve.

The patient should be treated much as he was before the stroke. Retaining his previous status and dignity in the family helps him to regain confidence. He should be included in conversations and never be spoken about as though he were absent. He should be allowed to answer for himself as best he can.

RECOVERY AND REHABILITATION

Once a stroke has occurred the most important step is the development of a rehabilitation program. All people are not equally affected by strokes. While some are only slightly affected others make a quick recovery from what seemed like a severe stroke. There are those who take an extended time period to regain even partial use of their limbs, speech, or whatever faculty has been affected.

Rehab is necessary for any patient who has paralysis and/or speech problems. Even those who are severely paralyzed may make progress towards becoming self-sufficient. For a successful rehabilitation the rehab program must begin as soon after the stroke as possible; the family should be the patient's chief support; the rehab program must be a team effort with all specialists working with the patient and his family.

Early rehabilitation measures such as frequent turning and positioning of the patient in bed and exercising paralyzed muscles should begin as soon as possible. These simple measures improve circulation, maintain joint flexibility, and prevent other complications from being confined to bed.[17]

Initially the nurse and/or therapist cares for the patient. Later the family is taught how to provide care. The goal is to have the patient achieve as much independence as possible.

The family is the most important resource during the rehab process. The patient must have the will to recover and the desire to be independent. So the family member closest to the patient will be involved with finding the most effective way of motivating him. Only family members can reassure the patient that he is wanted and needed and still has an important place in the family unit.[18]

EFFECT ON THE FAMILY

The patient is not the only person affected by the stroke. The impact on the family is great and the adjustment period may be difficult for both family and patient. Families need to be educated to know to what extent the patient has been affected and what they have to face as a result of his illness. Then realistic goals can be set.

Because the patient may have emotional upsets, known as emotional lability, the family has to be educated to the fact that these outbursts of inappropriate tears, laughter, or irritability are due to the stroke and not his feelings. These outbursts should not be taken personally nor should the patient be severely criticized or nagged.

Periods of depression are common. Due to slow progress the patient may become discouraged and indifferent to re-learning skills. He is overly sensitive and may become suspicious of what others are thinking and saying about him. For this reason he needs constant encouragement.

Sometimes a patient's judgment may be impaired and he may have memory lapses. In spite of these losses he may be mentally alert and capable in other respects. These changes may cause anxiety for the family. At such times they should talk to the doctor to understand the physiology of the behavior and to a chaplain or social worker to resolve their own difficulties.

Resolving the conflicts which an altered personality may create in a household is a difficult task but it can be accomplished. Giving the patient some responsibility and something to live for is half the battle. Families can also help the patient develop new interests which are within his capacities.

When the patient is aphasic it is important for the family to realize the patient can still think and, therefore, he should be included in decision making, especially about issues that involve him. Because his understanding is good it is better not to say anything near the patient that he shouldn't hear.

The duties of caring for the patient should be divided so that the burden of care does not fall on one member. The patient should be helped to take responsibility for regularly exercising and for self-care. It is an art to encourage independence and avoid frustration; to stimulate progress and not encourage unrealistic expectations. It is easier to praise his success and more difficult to avoid discouragement at his failures. Recovery is a slow process.

PERSONALITY PROBLEMS

Initially the patient may seem like himself. In the early stages he usually has a feeling of well-being. He appears to be happy, nothing worries him, and he has no concern for the future. As he is confronted with more and more situations he cannot cope with he retreats and adapts and his attitude and personality change.

The stroke patient tends to become self-centered and expects his needs to be cared for immediately. Emotional or impulsive behavior presents a problem. He throws things, pushes dishes off the table, physically or verbally abuses those around him.

Another difficulty confronting him is lack of initiative. He never remembers to do things for himself but must be constantly reminded. This includes the so-called simple chores such as brushing teeth and drinking water.

A condition that may be called "one track thinking" frequently is an annoying characteristic.[19] He will not let go of an idea until he has made it clear to others what it is he wants whether it takes a few minutes, a few hours, or a few days. This tenacity helps him during rehab when he is trying to master a skill. He will persist regardless of how long it takes.

The patient's attention span is short and his memory is not perfect. So he tends to ask for the same information day after day and repeats the same story. This is because long term memory is better than short term memory.

Abstract ideas are impossible to grasp and stories must be told with objects or actions. If the story is long he loses interest. Concentration may be beyond his ability and he is easily distracted. When his attention is held to one thing for several minutes he tires.

The inability to make himself understood and the sudden loss of his physical abilities are frustrating. He is dependent on others and can't say what he is thinking. It is not surprising then that the patient withdraws, loses interest, and becomes depressed.

Few patients are free from these spells but their frequency and length vary from patient to patient and from time to time in the same patient. The depressed patient stares into space, has fits of crying, refuses to eat or drink, and becomes irritable when disturbed. The depression has physical effects — legs drag, arms become useless, speech goes, bowels won't move.

Because of this physical and mental dependence, the patient begins to revert to childlike behavior. He is dominated by his emotions and loses his inhibitions. He cries from pain, openly displays his dislike for certain people and may even expose himself to show scars from surgical procedures.

It takes time, direction, and patience to help him return to adult behavior. A good sense of humor is also necessary. Laughing when you feel like crying or shouting will help. Becoming emotionally upset worsens the situation.

As physical improvement becomes evident attitude problems may remain. Frustration remains because the patient is not able to get around as well as he wants. Not feeling as tired as before he has more time to think and to want to do what he is not yet capable of. He still continues to be self-centered and emotionally unstable. His inhibitions remain.

As conditions improve the patient realizes he has a future and is willing to work toward it. His attention span is lengthened and it is easier to teach him. Past memory returns and this causes him to worry about the future.

Self-pity begins early and leads to depression if indulged in for long. Being unable to make decisions it is better to offer him choices that require only acquiescence.[20] However, the patient is perfectly capable of thinking up something he wants to do or has done for himself. Once his decision is made it must be done his way and he will insist until it is done his way.

Demands for immediate action are frequent.[21] He wants things done immediately with no consideration for others. If he feels he can disturb or dominate those around him there is no reason for him to stop. If his behavior has no appreciable effect he will adapt more acceptable behavior.

Another common development occurs rather unexpectedly. The patient's imagination runs wild and he begins telling fantastic tales.

Since this is not expected of an adult, the patient may have a whole family in an uproar over tales he tells each one about the other. When listening to a child it is easy to detect the imaginary tales a child tells as he lives in a world of fantasy. This is not so easy with the patient as he has the knowledge and memories of an adult to draw from for his tales. [22]

People tend to avoid someone who is sick and not his usual self because it hurts to see him. So the patient feels neglected and tries to get attention any way he can. Rousing people against each other may give him a sense of power. His imagination develops to the point where he is suspicious of and hostile toward those around him.

For much the same reason he complains constantly of small physical discomforts — itchy eyes, runny nose, constipation, sore throat — anything for attention. It is difficult to determine if these complaints have any merit. In making a determination the matter should not be unduly fussed about.

Love is necessary for a happy life. It can supply a tremendous amount of motivation. Love of self is the first love we experience. A stroke completely shatters one's self-image. A man prides himself in what he can do. A woman prides herself in being beautiful and desirable. A stroke destroys these feelings. The patient himself finds it impossible to love a person who is only half there, so it follows, in his mind, that no one could possibly love him. [23]

His first task is to build an acceptable self-image; then to learn to love both himself and others, and to accept love.

EMOTIONAL ADAPTATION

Suddenly becoming disabled is an emotionally overwhelming experience. When a person suffers a blow to the integrity of his body resulting in a loss of function, the grief is similar to losing a loved one or being told you have a terminal illness. Helping the patient through the grieving process is as much a part of rehabilitation as is physical therapy. How well the patient gets through the grieving process depends in part on his premorbid personality and in part on the reactions of family, friends, and caregivers.

Elisabeth Kübler-Ross has described the grieving process. *Denial* is the refusal to accept the facts. This is exhibited by the hemiplegic who tries to walk or insists the condition is temporary.

As time passes and the condition remains the patient begins to experience *anger* at his condition. This anger is focused on the caregivers who are asking for what seems impossible. Anger is exhausting but does nothing to change the condition.

At this point the patient may find himself making *bargains* with God or the caregivers. As the reality begins to dawn, *depression* sets in. The patient begins to feel hopeless, helpless, and worthless. This is the time he make remarks about dying.

Gradually as small tasks are mastered, he begins to feel less helpless and hope appears. Depression begins to lift and there is a gradual *acceptance* of reality.

As the depression lessens more energy is available for the rehab process. Motivation and perseverance are evident as the individual begins learning to adapt.

The grief process does not occur in any orderly manner. A major factor in working through the process is the impact of the disability on the patient's self-image. What does it mean to be confined to a wheelchair; to have leg and arm muscles atrophied; to wear a brace; to be dependent on others for personal needs such as washing, dressing, elimination?

The patient does not exist in a vacuum. He is part of a social system. The members of this social system also experience grief. Messages from these sources determine to a large extent how the patient will adapt. The spouse may be repulsed, horrified, or disgusted at the sight of the patient's condition, giving a message that he is no longer lovable. Role reversal may be necessary.

Added to the stress is the fact that the patient is hospitalized, away from his environment, and has no control. Caregivers decide what he will do and when he will do it. He is in a strange bed with side rails up. He is told to use his call bell — if he can find it, if he can remember it's there, and if he can reach it.

A major curative factor in dealing with emotional pain is the existence of a consistent, helping relationship that is safe and dependable.[24] It is within the safety of a trusting relationship that communication can be encouraged and feelings expressed. Some of these feelings come out as despair and rage that are not to be taken personally. These feelings should be investigated so the patient learns that his feelings are valid.

A consistent routine should be established to help the patient develop a sense of safety and security. This consistency allows the patient to feel accepted even in the face of failure and reduces the fear of being abandoned.

ROLE OF THE CHAPLAIN

The spiritual needs of the frail and disabled are often awesome, perplexing, and elusive. The mystery of spirituality has been reduced to the problematic, rendering it a problem to resolve rather than an opportunity and mystery to decipher and contemplate.[25] Religious concerns and beliefs evolve from and respond to mysteries of life and death, good and evil, and suffering. Organized religion offers various interpretations of these mysteries but most persons will seek their own meaning. Spirituality is the search to discover a unifying truth that will give meaning and purpose and integrity to our existence.

Each and every person searches for a truth that will support the significance of his life. To be human is to seek fulfillment in God or truth. James Fowler writes that our "god values" are those things that concern us ultimately. That ultimate concern may center finally in our own ego or its extensions—work, prestige, and recognition, power, influence, and wealth.[26]

Religious experience is an individualized quality. Spirituality grows out of each person's unique life experience. It follows then that pastoral care must acknowledge and respond to the needs of each person. It seeks to assist persons in discovering their God and their own understandings and interpretations of the events in their lives. For this reason the chaplain must deal with people within the context of their situation.

The goal of pastoral care is not to impose religious beliefs but to encourage and facilitate the spiritual pursuit. When a person struggles with the meaning of life and death and comes to an understanding, appreciation, and interpretation of these mysteries he arrives at serenity and resolve.

The problems of the stroke patient are chronic. As he struggles to find the meaning of disability and of death the chaplain's role is to help him discover something that will render his life meaningful.

The chaplain provides an intervention that is radically different from any other form of care. Other caregivers use their knowledge and expertise to alleviate pain and suffering and to ameliorate the personal, social, and economic problems of the disabled. They have a multitude of skills, technologies, and techniques to be used for the patient's benefit.

For the chaplain, whose primary task is to respond to the spiritual and religious needs, the most effective tool is his/her humanity. What the chaplain offers is not a system of beliefs or answers to someone's questions but the capacity and willingness to care, to listen, and to share in the struggles of another human being. The essence of spiritual intervention is not a professional response but a personal one. The chaplain offers himself/herself.

Knowledge and technology alone are insufficient to respond to the vast array of human needs. When technology is exhausted the spiritual and religious needs and concerns become illumined. The only remaining issue is the need of the patient for personal support, belonging, integrity, and discovering the meaning of life.

There are no quick solutions. The chaplain cannot propose a logical or theoretical resolution to a patient's search for meaning for his life. Such a resolution must be discovered by the patient.

Spiritual intervention is not a response but a sharing in the suffering of another. The resources the chaplain has to draw upon in being present to the suffering person are found in his/her personality and commitment to those being cared for. Sharing in someone's religious concerns requires the investment and commitment of one's self in the life of another. Only in this kind of relationship will the patient risk confronting the meaning of his life, death, and suffering.

Spirituality is not a problem to be solved but a mystery to be contemplated. It is important that one's life reflects the possibilities of hope, of meaning, of purpose, of God. Who I am and what I am willing to share will make the final difference in someone's spiritual life.

NOTES

1. *Strokes: A Guide for the Family*, American Heart Association, p. 3
2. Ibid., p. 6
3. Ibid., p. 9
4. *Stroke: Why Do They Behave That Way?*, American Heart Association, p. 5
5. Ibid., p. 6
6. Ibid., p. 7
7. Ibid., p. 9
8. Ibid., p. 11
9. Ibid., p. 12
10. Ibid., p. 12
11. Ibid., p. 17
12. Ibid., p. 26
13. Ibid., p. 28
14. Ibid., p. 28
15. *Aphasia and the Family*, American Heart Association, p. 3
16. Ibid., p. 8
17. Ibid., p. 12
18. Ibid., p. 12
19. *Care of the Patient With a Stroke*, p. 50
20. Ibid., p. 55
21. Ibid., p. 55
22. Ibid., p. 56
23. Ibid., p. 61
24. *Rehabilitation Nursing*, Sept./Oct. 84, p. 36
25. *Topics in Geriatric Rehabilitation — Spiritual Intervention Reconsidered*, p. 77
26. *Stages of Faith*, p. 4
   Biblical quotes are from *The New American Bible*

REFERENCES

1. American Heart Association. *Aphasia and the Family*. 1968.
2. American Heart Association. *Facts About Strokes*. 1968.
3. American Heart Association. *Stand Up to Stroke*. 1975.
4. American Heart Association. *Strokes: A Guide for the Family*. 1981.
5. Boyd, Jane, RN. "Differentiation of Right Hemiplegia-Left Brain Damage and Left Hemiplegia-Right Brain Damage," 1982.
6. Boyd, Jane, RN. "The Pieces — How They Fall, Stroke and Rehabilitation." 1982.
7. Boyd, Jane, RN. "Assessment and Management of the Stroke Patient." 1983.

8. Carr, Janet and Shepherd, Roberta. *Physiotherapy in Disorders of the Brain.* William Heinemann Medical Books Limited. London.
9. Cheney, Ruth Johnson, RN, MS. "Emotional Adaptation to Disability." *Rehabilitation Nursing.* Sept.-Oct. 84.
10. Cluff, Claudia, M. Div. "Spiritual Intervention Reconsidered." *Topics in Geriatric Rehabilitation.* Jan. 1986.
11. Dunn, Sally, RN. "An Education Program About Stroke," *Rehabilitation Nursing.* Sept.-Oct. 1984.
12. Fowler, James, *Stages of Faith.* Harper & Row. San Francisco. 1981.
13. Fowler, Roy, PhD and Fordyse, W. E., PhD. *Stroke: Why Do They Behave That Way?* American Heart Association. 1974.
14. Mahoney, Florence, MD and Barthel, Dorothea, BA, PT. *Up and Around.* American Heart Association.
15. Smith, Genevieve Waples, RN, MA. *Care of the Patient With a Stroke — Meeting Personality Problems.* Springer Publishing Co. New York.

The Use of Volunteer Community Clergy as Hospital Pastoral Care Staff

Dale E. Guckenberger, MDiv

SUMMARY. Review of six ongoing pastoral care programs which make extensive use of volunteer community clergy as Associate Chaplains indicating details of recruitment, orientation, training, volunteer benefits, cost of operation, Associate Chaplain duties, and program design. The pastoral care programs are operating in hospitals with from 227 to 498 beds and which have at least one full-time paid chaplain.

INTRODUCTION

With the onset of DRGs and the resulting economic pressure placed on health care institutions affected by the tax reform act of 1984, pastoral care departments in many hospitals have been forced to cut budgets and, at the same time, maintain a high level of ministry. Some hospitals have chosen to delete their programs. Others have developed creative ways of providing the necessary pastoral care for patients, staff, and families. One effective way of continuing to meet the religious and spiritual needs of the patients, staff, and families is with the use of volunteer community clergy as "Associate Chaplains." While there is some expense involved in the use of volunteers in the hospital setting, it is much less than the cost of full- or part-time paid staff. This author has reviewed six programs which use volunteer community clergy as an integral part of their pastoral care departments. All of these programs include at least one full-time paid chaplain and between twenty-four and sev-

Dale E. Guckenberger, Chaplain and Director of Pastoral Care, La Porte Hospital, P.O. Box 250, La Porte, IN 46350-0250.

enty volunteer "Associate Chaplains." The hospitals range in size from 227 to 498 beds. Volunteers in the programs reviewed represent a wide range of denominational backgrounds including "mainline" Protestant, conservative Protestant, Roman Catholic and Jewish clergy.

The data for this review was gathered from personal correspondence with Frank M. Brown, Research Medical Center, Kansas City, Missouri; Barry K. Durie, St. Luke's Hospital of Bethlehem, Pennsylvania; and Richard B. Gilbert, Burlington Medical Center, Burlington, Iowa; and from presentations made by William H. Price, Lexington County Hospital, West Columbia, South Carolina; Gordon E. Johnston, Ellis Hospital, Schenectady, New York; and the author, La Porte Hospital, La Porte, Indiana, at the Special Interest Group on Use of Volunteer Clergy for the 1987 meeting of the College of Chaplains in New Orleans, Louisiana. The details outlined in this review are a compilation of the data gathered from these sources.

The title "Associate Chaplain" has been chosen for this review, though the position has been referred to in some of the programs as "Night Chaplain" or "Reserve Chaplain." The position of Associate Chaplain refers to a volunteer community clergy recognized by the hospital chaplain as a pastor or other clergy serving in the community. Two of the programs also included lay volunteer chaplains. Their function will not be reviewed in this paper.

RECRUITMENT AND TRAINING
OF ASSOCIATE CHAPLAINS

Qualifications for Associate Chaplains

In all of the programs reviewed, the basic qualifications for Associate Chaplain included ordination or recognition by the clergy person's denomination or faith group. The person's faith group may be a denomination, local congregation, or other official body to which the clergy is currently responsible. In all of the programs the individual was interviewed by the chaplain or Director of Pastoral Care with specific discussion focusing on their concern for people, pastoral care skills, willingness to receive supervision as an Associate

Chaplain, interest in learning new skills and availability to participate in ongoing education for Associate Chaplains within the structure of the hospital in which they would be serving. Their availability to serve as Associate Chaplain within the scheduled framework of the hospital was also a qualifying factor. Two of the programs specifically indicated a "trial" period during which the Associate Chaplain would be monitored very closely by the chaplain. One program stipulated a trial night on-call and a trial week on duty. Another program required personal briefing and debriefing with the chaplain for the first three months of active service. One of the programs required a review by an Executive Committee of Associate Chaplains of each new recruit.

Recruitment of Associate Chaplains

The recruiting process was similar in all of the programs. New Associate Chaplains were recruited from those indicating interest in serving and from those sought out by the chaplain or Director of Pastoral Care. The impression of the author is that all Associate Chaplains were hand-picked by their respective directors much as a paid staff person would be selected.

Orientation, Training, and Continuing Education of Associate Chaplains

There is wide variety in the orientation and training provided the Associate Chaplains. The following outlines from the various hospitals indicate the variety of training provided.

La Porte Hospital

The newly recruited Associate Chaplain participates once in the day-long monthly new employee orientation program. Following this event the Associate Chaplain is guided through a special tour of the hospital by the chaplain where specific and necessary parts of the facility are identified and during which the new Associate Chaplain is introduced to key hospital personnel including nurses, physicians, nurse managers, and others with whom the Associate Chaplain may be working during their duty times.

Following this general orientation there is specific instruction in the use of the hospital paging system, record keeping for pastoral care and "in-house housekeeping" procedures. During subsequent briefing and debriefing sessions held prior to the Associate Chaplain's duty time, specific topics like death, code blue, and trauma procedures are outlined as necessary. This briefing and debriefing procedure continues for three to four months. There are periodic seminars held for the Associate Chaplains as a group throughout the year. These seminars focus on topics which will apply directly to the responsibilities of the Associate Chaplain.

St. Luke's Hospital of Bethlehem

There is a monthly two hour Associate Chaplain group during which clinical materials are shared by Associate Chaplains on a rotating basis.

Lexington County Hospital

The pastoral care department provides monthly breakfasts with educational speakers. In addition to the monthly breakfasts the chaplain meets daily for lunch with the Associate Chaplain on duty for schedule planning, review, supervision and training. There are also ongoing support groups of four to five Associate Chaplains each.

Ellis Hospital

Initially orientation was done as a group of Associate Chaplains. As the program has developed the orientation has been done on an individual basis. Training is also provided by the hospital staff and by outside specialists from the local area. For instance if there is a "Cancer Chaplain" in the area s/he would present information from that area of specialty.

BENEFITS PROVIDED FOR ASSOCIATE CHAPLAINS

There is again a wide range of benefits provided the Associate Chaplains. The list below is a compilation from the data gathered from the programs reviewed:

— free meals in the hospital cafeteria while on duty
— employee prescription service
— hospital provided educational opportunities
— consultation with the chaplain
— learn about the hospital, its mission, and future plans
— computer print-out for their own congregation of hospitalized members
— special parking privileges
— free lodging while on duty
— participation in hospital day care program for sick children

RESPONSIBILITIES OF ASSOCIATE CHAPLAINS

The Associate Chaplains in the programs reviewed are on duty in the following patterns.

Lexington County

This program has seventy Associate Chaplains who serve for one full week once a year. They are in the hospital to have lunch with the chaplain and visit patients from one to four hours a day Monday through Friday and on call from 5:00 p.m. until 8:00 a.m. the following morning. If there are evenings which they cannot cover because of other responsibilities the chaplain takes the on-call time. These Associate Chaplains carry a pager. They do not stay overnight in the hospital.

Ellis Hospital

This program has thirty-five Associate Chaplains who serve one night a month. During their duty time these Associate Chaplains may stay in the hospital. They will make pre-operative visits, respond to traumas in the emergency room, answer "code blue" calls, and follow up patients from the day chaplain. At times these Associate Chaplains are asked to fill in for local pastors who are unable to come to the hospital for traumas, deaths, or other emergencies.

Burlington Medical Center

These Associate Chaplains informally fill in for the chaplain when he has to be away from the hospital.

Research Medical Center

The twenty-five Associate Chaplains provide on-call coverage three to four nights a year supplementing the on-call coverage provided by the six CPE students. They stay in the hospital and are on duty from 4:30 p.m. until 8:00 a.m. the following morning. They carry a pager. Their duties during their on-call time include responding to referrals from hospital staff, making rounds on the intensive care unit and emergency room, pre-operative visits, being with families when death has occurred and providing the Sacraments of Baptism and Holy Communion when requested.

St. Luke's Hospital of Bethlehem

The twenty-five Associate Chaplains serve one night per month on call from 5:00 p.m. until 8:00 a.m. the following morning.

La Porte Hospital

The twenty-four Associate Chaplains serve one to two nights per month "on-call" carrying a long distance pager which allows them to be reached within a fifteen mile radius of the hospital. Three of this group stay overnight in the hospital. Duties include responding to deaths in the hospital, traumas in the emergency room and "code blue" calls. They may also be asked to make pre-operative visits. The Associate Chaplains who stay overnight in the hospital may also be asked to follow up on patients seen during the day or make visits on patients not reached during the day by the chaplain.

COST OF OPERATING
A VOLUNTEER CLERGY PROGRAM

In neither the personal correspondence nor the presentations made in New Orleans was cost raised as a specific issue. The data available to this author is from his own program in La Porte Hospital. The cost of the La Porte Hospital Associate Chaplain program includes the following ongoing expenses:

- meals for on duty Associate Chaplains (approximately $10/ month)
- chaplain's time for supervision, training, and administration is approximately 20 hours per month
- there is no amount charged to the Pastoral Care department budget for use of the guest room when the Associate Chaplain stays overnight
- clerical work required for the program is provided by volunteers
- the only additional expense was for a long distance pager specifically for the Associate Chaplain

DISCUSSION

All of the programs which have been cited in this review are currently operating successfully, one for over fifteen years. Two of the programs are monitored by a group in addition to the chaplain or the department director.

It has been the experience of the author that this monitoring body is supportive and encouraging, at least as it has operated at La Porte Hospital. During the discussions in New Orleans, a variety of questions and issues were raised by the group interested in the use of community clergy. One question raised asked if there was a threat to non-participating community clergy by the presence of the Associate Chaplain. None of the presenters had experienced any such concerns in their own programs. Another question focused on the possible problem of proselytizing of patients by Associate Chaplains. It was clearly indicated in each of the programs reviewed in New Orleans that this issue was dealt with during training and orientation and did not appear as a problem during the operation of the program.

In the La Porte Hospital program there is a strong emphasis on involving the patient/family's pastor in their pastoral care. Associate Chaplains are encouraged to contact the patient/family's pastor whenever possible and defer all pastoral care to that pastor. This emphasis on the supportive nature of the Associate Chaplain has received expressed appreciation from most community clergy. There are of course those who would rather not be bothered in the middle of the night with a hospital crisis, but Associate Chaplains are instructed to phone the pastor in any event of death, code blue, or trauma.

The distinct advantage as seen from this review is a program of pastoral care that can be provided with a single full-time chaplain and minimal additional expense. The involvement of the volunteer Associate Chaplains encourages a bonding between community clergy and the hospital. It also encourages hospital staff to relate in a more interested and personal way to the clergy who visit their own patients as well as serve as Associate Chaplains. The Associate Chaplain programs provide an alternate form of ministry for many pastors as well as offering them specific benefits which otherwise would not be available to them. There are administrative details which are beyond the scope of this review which are available from the author, namely report forms, scheduling procedures, hospital and Associate Chaplain notification processes. Interested readers may write to Dale E. Guckenberger, Chaplain, La Porte Hospital, P.O. Box 250, La Porte, IN 46350-0250.